AN OWNER'S GUIDE TO
FATHERHOOD

LIVING WITH CHILDREN
AND OTHER CREATURES

CHRIS EWING

PROMISE
PRESS
An Imprint of Barbour Publishing

AN OWNER'S GUIDE TO
FATHERHOOD

Published by Promise Press, an imprint of Barbour Publishing, Inc., P.O. Box 719, Uhrichsville, Ohio 44683, http://www.barbourbooks.com

 Member of the
Evangelical Christian
Publishers Association

Printed in the United States of America.

Preface

*"People were bringing little children
to Jesus to have him touch them,
but the disciples rebuked them.
When Jesus saw this, he was indignant.
He said to them, 'Let the little children come to me,
and do not hinder them,
for the kingdom of God belongs to such as these.'"*
MARK 10:13–14

When it comes to being a father, I probably make more mistakes than not. That is just the nature of being a male and attempting to interact with children. It really is an experimental process. Oh, sure, there are a hundred books out there on raising children, but after trying these great ideas out, it always comes down to the same thing: There is no "owner's guide" to being a parent. What easily works for one person may be impossible or disastrous for another. Today's innovative fad is tomorrow's big mistake. There are no set instructions, no wondrous formula to insure that your children will grow up to be intelligent, healthy adults or that you will retain any shred of sanity that you once thought you may have had.

That is the magic of children. They always manage to keep you on your toes and keep your mind churning to be one step ahead of the game. And it is amazing how often you are lulled into a false sense of superiority and comfort. Just when you think you have some tiny bit of insight into life or some problem solved, a kid throws your best monkey wrench into the works and you have to start from scratch. Above it all, however, is a sort of divine beauty and, if you let yourself experience it, a wondrous rediscovery of youth—the give and the take, the mundane and the special, the heartache and the joy.

So why *An Owner's Guide to Fatherhood*? Maybe because no one ever talks about the approach men, those "Mars" guys, take to parenting. There is a definite difference between how men and women view raising children, although I'm not so sure it is something that you can verbalize well nor is it something you should brag about. It has nothing to do with the level of our feelings toward our offspring or agreeing with our spouses on how to raise the little rascals. I'd like to think, however, that while mothers may give the lion's share of nurturing, fathers, somehow, impart to their children strength and hope and humor.

For instance, when a child comes home beat up and bruised and says he got in a fight after school because some kid was picking on him, mothers see the blood and tears and excitedly say, "Are you all right?" Fathers see that the child is alive and more or less functional and are more prone to calmly drawl, "Did ya win?" Kids need this kind of reinforcement every now and then.

I once took a spur-of-the-moment survey of the neighborhood kids and a few of their fathers to get a better idea on what was expected of male parents. From my informal poll, I gleaned the following tidbits of wisdom.

The Ideal Father should be independently wealthy. This allows his family to have whatever their misguided hearts would desire. An unlimited supply of toys, televisions, automobiles, and computer games. . .a huge abode with several rooms for every resident—including, of course, a private bathroom for everyone. . .oh, yes—let us not forget the maid.

I do not now, nor have I ever, possessed a measurable net worth.

The Ideal Father should not be gainfully employed (see above) or have hobbies of his own devising. This allows the hapless chap to be at the beck and call of his children, playing with and entertaining them twenty-four hours a day.

I am not currently (praise the Lord!) unemployed.

The Ideal Father should never get sick or tired or grouchy or worried. All of these conditions detract from the "quality" time he can spend with his offspring. Let us not forget that this same man must have the patience and attributes of a number of well-known saints.

I am not, by any definition, a saint.

What, then, is the definition of an Ideal Father?

I wouldn't have the foggiest idea.

This is a subject we must all struggle with and personalize to best suit our temperament and the personalities of our individual family members. I would humbly suggest, however, that instead of trying to achieve "saintdom" in your children's eyes, which isn't going to happen anyway, you might just settle for doing "the best you can."

If you really have a burning desire to know what an Ideal Father is, and I highly recommend against this course of inquiry, ask your kids.

The responsibilities of effective parenting are legion. I know I could never have gotten to where I am—and I'm still not exactly sure where that is—alone. I have neither the fortitude nor the intelligence. Growing up is a lifelong communal activity and helping this process along will take all the resources and determination you can beg, borrow, or steal and all the faith and love that God can give. Maybe that is why the word "father" appears an even fifteen hundred times in the Bible.

Even though it is almost impossible to define, being a father is an undeniably strenuous and demanding occupation that should not be taken lightly.

Or maybe it should. . . .

Incomplete Information

"Train a child in the way he should go,
and when he is old he will not turn from it."
PROVERBS 22:6

It is my own fault, I suppose. Trying to instill a quest for learning in my children has led to my current sorry position of being in a growing state of educational inequality. In other words, I have reached the point where there are more questions I can't answer than there are ones that I can.

Remember the nursery rhyme "Twinkle, Twinkle Little Star"? I changed it for my children, to help foster the pursuit of science.

Twinkle, twinkle little star,
How I wonder what you are.
Hydrogen gases swirling above,
Fusion fires that consume all love.
Twinkle, twinkle little star,
Now we know just what you are.

My daughter asked, "Dad, if superconducting electromagnets generate magnetic fields millions of times stronger than the earth's, how come that doesn't mess up everyone's compasses?"

Hmm. Good question! Now being a male and not wanting to display my ignorance in front of the children, I struggled for a plausible answer.

"Uh, well, by international law, I believe it is United Nations Mandate 4061, section 4, paragraph 13, and I quote, 'All large magnets, be they electrical in nature or not, must be installed so their magnetic poles align with those of the earth.' That keeps everything in sync, so there is no conflict in magnetic fields and all compasses remain pointing to their true polar direction." Whew!

"Oh. Wow, Dad, you sure are smart!"

The really tough questions, however, come from the youngest minds.

"Daddy, what makes clouds?"

No problemo, I think.

"Well, when water evaporates, it rises into. . ."

"Daddy, what's 'vaporates' mean?"

"E-vap-or-ates. That is when water turns into a vapor, which is kind of like a gas, and it goes into the air."

"Gas like you put in the car? From the gas 'tation?"

"Well, not really. The gas you put in the car is a liquid, like water." I involuntarily wince at the memory of catching some youngster trying to fill the car's gas tank with the garden hose. "But we will not EVER try to put water in the car again, will we?" I reinforced.

"Okay," he said.

Sure. Right.

"Anyway, there are also gases that are like air. You just can't see them because the molecules are so far apart that they are invisible and you can see right through them."

"What are mol-kules?"

"Those are the little tiny pieces that make up everything in the world."

"Even me?"

"Even you."

"But will I become in-divisible?"

This conversation had, as usual, rapidly gotten out of control.

"What?" I asked.

"Indivisible. So you can't see me anymore. Like the air."

Oh.

"No, you don't get to be invisible until you are five years old."

A shocked expression flashed across his face.

"Kidding, just kidding," I quickly reassured. "You won't become invisible."

"But I want to be in-divisible!" he whined.

"Sorry! Sorry I tried to be nice and explain something to you! Now, do you want to know about clouds or not?"

"Yes," he sighed. "That is what I have been wanting and wanting!"

"All right. Clouds are just water that floats up in the air.

When they get too much water in them, it rains or snows."

"Oh."

"And when clouds come down to the ground, that is fog."

That perked him up.

"Then we get to drive in a cloud?"

"That's right."

"Cool!"

Sheesh. What it takes to get through to some people.

I spent much of my youth in the rocket age. What a wonderful time for a kid's imagination to be fertilized, so to speak. There were the Redstones and Geminis and Saturn boosters and Apollo missions. It was all so wonderful and exciting and ended up as the seed that germinated into my lifelong appreciation for science.

I'll never forget the excitement of getting my mail-order model rocket kits in the mail. I would be so anxious to blast to the heavens that I would rush through the assembly, cutting and gluing the balsa wood fins onto the slender cardboard tubes. I'd paint everything bright colors and triple check the parachute operation before rushing out with my new wonder to my homemade launching pad in the driveway. I'd put in a solid-fuel propellant engine, those tiny marvels of force and power, count down from five, and travel halfway to the stars in a matter of three seconds of glorious smoke and fire and noise.

I'll also never forget the time I fired up a particularly sleek beauty just to have it rise ten feet above the ground, shed its fins, make a sharp right-angle turn, and career into the side of the garage—all in the allotted three seconds of maximum thrust. Talk about sudden impact! All I ever found were two of the three fins at the launch site and some shredded plastic I assumed was the remains of the parachute.

I guess I should've let the glue dry longer.

As an adult, you learn from these childhood experiences and share that knowledge with your children. Naturally, when they were old enough, I bought model rockets for my kids. But the excitement just wasn't there for them. Growing up with computers and video games and instant anything somehow took a little of the edge off that wonder we call science. The kits took too long to assemble (yes, Virginia, you actually have to read instructions!). At least I still get a reasonable amount of satisfaction and excitement when I put the rockets together for them.

I vividly recall this one particular beauty, however, that I bought for my kids. It was so sleek and fast-looking, it had me reliving my childhood. I rushed through the assembly, cutting and gluing the balsa wood fins onto the slender cardboard tube. I painted everything bright colors and triple-checked the parachute operation before rushing out with my new wonder to my homemade launching pad in the field beside the house. I put in a solid-fuel propellant engine, those tiny marvels of force and power, and backed off. Five-four-three-two-one-ignition!

It was with an uncanny sense of déjà vu that I watched my creation shed its fins, make a sharp right-angle turn, and careen into the side of the garage—all in the allotted three seconds of maximum thrust. I learned three things from that particular flight: I should have let the glue dry longer, they don't make garages like they used to, and the way history repeats itself can be downright unsettling.

I confess that I am not a very good teacher. My patience and perseverance just aren't quite as good as they should be. It takes a special person to be able to communicate effectively with children, especially small children. Oh, I try to spark the desire of learning. I point out interesting facts and figures, trivia meant to tantalize the mind for more substantial material. But when it comes to getting them really fired up about something, it just doesn't quite click sometimes.

If you have experienced the same, all I can say is, "Don't give up." We may not see the immediate benefits of our patient endeavors, but I firmly believe that the mental paths are being formed, paths that will help our children to eventually seek out truth and knowledge and goodness in a world full of uncertainty and confusion and laziness.

I recently attempted to assemble a toy my son had received for his birthday. In the instructions were words that made my blood run cold: "Some patience may be required. . . ." *Oh, great,* I thought. When something starts off like that, you instinctively know you are in trouble. And, as usual, the manufacturers understated the obvious. A LOT of patience was required and, even then, the finished product didn't quite turn out as expected. Seems I had left out a tiny little plastic piece which had rolled off the table and had been immediately gobbled up by the dog.

So it is with a family. "Some patience may be required. . ." is an understatement. An unbelievable amount of commitment, hard work, and love is required and things still never quite turn out as expected. We can just pray that the finished product is functional and durable and is something we can be proud of—even if a few little pieces have turned up missing.

Lord, guide me as I try to teach my children what is right and of the rightness and wonder of Your universe. I pray they will be receptive to Your word and will follow the paths that You have planned for them. Use me as a catalyst to help them grow in the grace of Jesus Christ.

Pet Peeves

> *"Now it is required that those who have been
> given a trust must prove faithful."*
> 1 CORINTHIANS 4:2

Pets can be a wonderful experience for your children. They can teach many lessons about life—responsibility, friendship, pain. They are a part of growing up and a part of learning about this wonderfully diverse world in which we live. Unfortunately, as a father, you must also be prepared for the downside of pet ownership. Here are a few of the possibilities you may (or may not) want to investigate.

Aquaticus Toileticus (Fish)

What can I say about goldfish? We tried them. Of course, we've tried everything. The kids said, in unison, "Dad, we want fish. All our friends have fish. Why can't we have fish?" No rehearsing here, nosiree.

"Fish sticks or fillets?" I asked. "Salmon or flounder?"

"Live fish, Dad. That swim in a tank."

Oh. That kind of fish.

"We have a cat. Cats eat fish. Besides," I added, "fish stink. They are cold and wet and they stink. And you can't cuddle up to them like a small, furry animal."

The kids brightened up.

"Can we have a hamster? We could get a boy hamster and a girl hamster and they could have babies and we could sell them and make lots of money! Pleeeese?"

"Let me see if that old fish tank is still in the garage attic."

Fish last longer if they are not cared for by little children who either (A) forget to feed them for days on end and wonder how come they're floating upside down, (B) feed them a third of the box of fish food and then wonder how come they're floating upside down, or (C) try to teach the fish how to high dive from the ceiling fan and then wonder how come they're floating upside down.

Toilet food.

The cat won't even eat them.

Chewitus Upitus (Small Furry Mammals)

You cannot have a cat and small, furry animals in the house at the same time. This just does not work. Of course, the children do not understand this concept and eventually you are dragged screaming and kicking from the house by the entire family and told you will not be allowed to return without a small, furry animal in tow. So we loaded up the car and headed off into the sunset to look for some obnoxious little rodent. I would have been glad to set a trap in the garden, but, no, that wasn't quite what they were looking for.

Luckily, the local discount store carried small, furry animals at a reduced price. Their habitat, however, came at a premium. I decided a shoe box would be sufficient. Who needs a high-rise plastic-and-metal condominium for a rat, anyway? Not to mention food, water bottles, bedding, chew toys, vitamins, etcetera.

So we went home and everyone agreed that the little hamster is cute and we built a nice little house for it and the kids went to sleep with smiles of contentment on their cherubic faces.

The next morning the cat was not hungry and the shoe box was empty and I found a cute little rodent foot under the kitchen table.

"Anyone want an unlucky rodent foot?"

No takers.

We went back to the discount store and got another little mammal and a high-rise plastic-and-steel condominium. I had to admit, this worked ever so much better than a shoe box. It was fun, at least for a while, to watch the little creature run through convoluted tunnels that never went anywhere and jog on his little hamster treadmill that had a squeak that could be heard throughout the house at two in the morning.

However, a warning about small, furry animals. They are escape artists and they are very curious. They will squeeze or eat their way through any opening just so they can get a closer look at, for instance, a cat. Little do they realize it will be their last look at a mammal higher up on the food chain than they are. These little rodents have been known to chew holes through doors to sacrifice themselves in this manner. We decided they must be part lemming or something and no longer feed our feline in this manner.

Felinus Aloofnus (Cats)

As any cat owner will attest, felines are a different kind of animal. They have always suited me as they require a minimum of attention and man and beast can generally just ignore each other. A few years back, however, we had a visitor that couldn't be ignored.

Late one night, I heard all kinds of strange sounds coming from our basement. Bumps. Thumps. I got out of bed and went down to investigate. I flipped on the light to the stairs to hear an immediate crash as something glass shattered. I grabbed the baseball bat behind the door and crept silently downward.

Someone, or some thing, was in the process of trashing the basement, which wasn't hard to do since it was used only for storage. Boxes lay scattered on the floor. The remains of a glass lamp lay in the corner. I crept onward and noticed an outside window was open a crack. Suddenly, like in a B horror movie, this blob of fur sprang out from behind the washing machine and went tearing across the floor.

A cat. Some unfortunate had gotten in through the

window and couldn't get out. Well, I'd better help him out before my kids saw the mangy creature and wanted to adopt it.

I advanced slowly toward the animal and noticed he didn't look too well. Some of us lead rougher lives than others, I guess.

"Here, kitty, kitty," I said soothingly. "Let me help you out."

I put the bat down so I could pick up the cat with both hands. With a yowl that made me jump, the cat suddenly attacked. I threw up my left hand to shield my face and throat. The cat grabbed onto the right. I stepped backward, tripped on the bat, and went down. Now the wild beast had the upper hand, so to speak, and pressed on with the attack, chewing like mad. I jumped up, screaming bloody murder, and finally managed to frantically shake the leech off my hand. He ran off into a corner, eyeing me and spitting and hissing. I ran off into the opposite corner, eyeing him and spitting and hissing and calculating the chances that I could reach the bat on the floor between us. It was a standoff.

My wife appeared at the top of the stairs.

"Do not come down!" I yelled. "There is a deranged monster down here! Shut the door and lock it behind you!"

"Really," she sleepily muttered as she shut the door. "You flatter yourself too much."

Click went the lock.

Now I was locked in with this creature. I wasn't in any mood for another encounter of the bloody kind, so I eased around to the basement door, the cat turning and spitting at me every foot of the way. I opened the outside door wide and backed off. It took awhile and I had to throw a number of boxes and articles of clothing at it before it finally got the idea and made a dash for freedom.

The doctor was very understanding as she administered a tetanus shot and sewed up my hand.

"And where is this creature now?" she asked.

"In some other state, I hope," I replied.

She thought a minute before continuing. "I'd like to discuss something with you, something that is fairly common around here—and extremely unpleasant."

I looked up at the sudden change in her voice.

"Let's talk rabies."

"I'll find the cat," I replied.

The neighbors thought I was nuts, creeping around the bushes at all hours of the day and night and meowing like a cat in heat. I left little cans of open cat food around the back door. I warned the children not to go outside or the "bogey-cat" would eat them. But my time was running out.

One sleepless night after dreaming dark dreams of werewolves, I checked the "catch-them-alive" trap at the back door. Bingo. One spitting, hissing ball of fury. He lived in the garage, well caged and well fed, until his (and my) ten-day sentence was up and then went to live with friends in the country.

The kids still get a kick out of my reenactment of the

whole fight scene. I take a stuffed toy cat and hold it up to my neck with both hands and struggle and gurgle with my eyes rolled back in their sockets. Then I tear it from my throat and fling it against the wall and beat on it with a pillow.

"And that's how it was," I pant.

The kids love it.

It seems like we have always had cats. Tame ones, though. Healthy to extremes. Our current feline is a wonderful example of aloofness. He is what you would call an "outdoor" cat since he spends most of his time out there hunting for anything that moves, protecting his territory, and getting the feathers beat out of him by other cats doing the same thing. That's what they do. He has notches in his ears like the Old West gunfighters had notches in their guns. Another fight, another notch. Pretty soon he won't have any ears at all.

Ruff (he used to have a brother named Tumble until Tumble got eaten by a coyote) does have a few peculiarities, however. One is that he meows to go out every night around three in the morning. You can set your clock by when he comes into the bedroom and jumps on your face to get your attention. His other endearing trait is that he meows constantly until he is fed, and if he doesn't get fed fast enough, he bites your feet to remind you he is down there wasting away. These are the only times you'll ever hear from him.

Of course, the kids really don't need small furry animals

as pets when you have a cat. Cats will bring lots of critters in various states of life to you. At least lots of parts. A wonderfully educational way for the children to learn anatomy. Nature at its best and all that.

"Eeeyuuu!" my older daughter exclaimed as she pointed to the corner of the yard. "What's that?"

"Hmm. Looks like a gopher. Big one. Can't be too sure without the head, though. I guess the cat was full. Say, why don't you go in the house and get the frying pan, would you, please?"

"Daaad!"

"Kidding, just kidding!" Man, she takes everything so literally!

"Let's bury it!"

"And dig up this beautifully manicured lawn? No way!" Like there weren't already holes in the yard big enough to set full-grown trees in.

"This is gross—I have to tell Mom." She took off. Anytime there is something gross to be seen, the kids have to show their mother because they like to see how fast her face turns white.

Better do something quick before I have to dig up the whole backyard. Hmm. I checked the back door. *Good, no witnesses.* Checked next door. *They have a cat, don't they? Yeah, they do! The one that always beats up on our cat. Perfect.*

I picked up the stiff little corpse by one little paw and expertly flung it over the fence into the neighbor's yard with a flick of my wrist.

About then, out came my daughter dragging my thoroughly disgusted spouse behind her.

"What are you going to do with the dead critter?" she wanted to know.

"What critter?" I replied. "There's something dead back here? Oh, gross!"

I could tell by her expression that my wife was not in the mood for this. "OK, OK. I already disposed of it. Can't have dead things lying around the yard, now can we? Might attract flies or something."

It was obvious that she was relieved as she turned and headed for the relative safety of the house.

"Eeeyuuu!" my older daughter exclaimed again, pointing to yet another corner of the yard. "What's that?"

Sigh.

I suppose it could be worse. We could have a dog.

Caninus Pesti-plenti-cuss (Dogs)

If you are a normal father, sooner or later you are going to consider getting a cute, adorable little puppy for a child of yours. The child will beg you and bother you and draw doggie pictures and sing doggie songs and promise to take care of it until you succumb to the constant, insidious brainwashing.

Don't give in.

Just say "no."

If you want that kind of pain, just go out to the garage, find a two-by-four, and start beating yourself on the head with it. It hurts just the same and is a lot less expensive. I know. Really. You see, I was brainwashed once.

I still don't know how it happened but, the first thing I knew, my wife and I were driving around town looking at dogs. We finally decided a puppy was in order and ended up getting a hound. The pup's mother was so calm and nice we knew this was the dog for us. Little did we know that the pup's father was a carrier of the dreaded Caninus Desperadus, a.k.a. the "doggy desperado," gene. We suspected this much after the dog grew. He had a strong voice—a hound voice, low but powerful, something akin to an old-fashioned train whistle. Carried for miles. Just ask anyone in the neighborhood. He also got big fast, bigger than his mom. And strong! This animal could yank me right off my feet and had no problem whatsoever in pulling the kids through cactus and rocks.

Now, this worried me somewhat, especially after the time Dog ran into Daughter headfirst during some especially rambunctious play. The *thunk* these two hard heads made coming together echoed all over the backyard. I ran over to help my daughter off the ground and was shocked by the true goose-egg bruise on her forehead and the glazed look in her eyes.

"How many fingers?" I asked as I held four of my digits up in front of her.

"How many who?" she asked.

"Fingers. On my hand."

She struggled in vain to focus.

"Eighteen? Say, who are you, anyway?"

From that time on, no one was allowed to be on the same level as Dog. This wasn't easy to enforce since he could also jump up and put his paws on my shoulders and, if he stood on tip-paws, look me square in the face with those big, mournful brown eyes. Who could resist?

But the love-hate relationship with this animal took an abrupt lean toward the latter when we went on a short trip and had a friend come over to feed, water, and play with our half-grown pup—who was living outside full time.

Our minivacation didn't go so well. It was one of those vacations where you wish you would have just gone and burned your money because it would have been more fun and less exhausting, if you know what I mean. I was really looking forward to getting back home so I could relax. But when we arrived home and I opened up the front door, who should greet us but Mr. Break-and-Enter Mutt.

"Uh, oh," I said.

I looked around the house.

"Oh. My."

I dropped the suitcases. My wife dropped hers. The kids dropped theirs. The dog continued to race up and down the stairs, barking incessantly and showing off what was left of all the great things he had discovered.

As far as we could piece together, this is what happened: After our friend had fed, watered, and played with the Destroyer and gone home, the dog had apparently pried the outside screen off one of the basement windows. He then proceeded to somehow open both the storm window and the inside window. He jumped into the house, knocking over and breaking a lamp. He ate the cat food. He drank from toilets. He scattered as much garbage as possible around the house. He ate the kids' stuffed animals. He ate the kids' plastic toys. Like Goldilocks, he tried everyone's chair and bed. He had to go to the bathroom. Any number of times. He opened the kitchen cupboards and ate my son's Koco-Krunchies and anything else he could find. He got sick. Several times.

What could I do?

I calmly put Destructo out in the backyard (what yard?) where he belonged, went out in the garage, and started beating myself on the head with a two-by-four.

It took a full day, a rented carpet shampooer, and a trip to the landfill before I could get the house close to its original condition. But it never has been quite the same.

Quackus Fowliticus (Ducks)

Ducks are nice. Ducks are funny. Ducks require very little care. They are better than a dog. They will eat your garden, but they will not eat your house. Besides, they make a great Thanksgiving dinner main course.

("Daaad!")

Above all, I have tried to instill in my children an attitude of respect and love for all living creatures. Every creature, from the lowly earthworm to the majestic whale, has its place on this fragile planet and in God's universe according to His divine plan. We, as stewards of these gifts, dare not abuse the trust that has been placed in us to humanely care for and use these creatures and the earthly environment we all share. As the hymn teaches us, "All things bright and beautiful, all creatures great and small, all things wise and wonderful, the Lord God made them all."

Dear Lord, Creator of life, help us become faithful stewards of the many gifts You have graciously given us. I try to conscientiously teach my children the place Your creatures have in the universe. And I will try to remember to rejoice with them in the diversity and beauty of the life that surrounds us every day.

Thin Insulation

"A fool spurns his father's discipline,
but whoever heeds correction shows prudence."
PROVERBS 15:5

Every good parent must make efficient use of insulation. Now there are several kinds of insulation that apply here and each is as important as the next, only in slightly different ways. Suffice it to say that without insulation, you would be in serious trouble (as if we parents weren't already).

Our houses are insulated to keep out the cold in the winter, the heat in the summer, and the wind (if you live in Chicago or Wyoming) all the rest of the time. Not only does this protective layer hopefully keep out the elements, but it also keeps some of them in, mainly noise. Our particular neighborhood greatly values the peace and quiet of a suburban setting, and every abode is required by city ordinance to have a minimum of three inches of soundproofing. This works pretty well, except the noise level within the house can sometimes exceed OSHA's limits, especially when everyone is home and supper is being prepared.

When you combine at least one stereo with at least one television with the banging of pots and pans and the probable practicing of large wind instruments and/or a piano and a ringing telephone. . .Well, I think you get the picture, and it isn't a pretty one. The number of decibels of pure, raw sound energy you are exposed to grows exponentially with the number of children within the building. It is this time of day and under these conditions when parents are most likely to flip out and do grievous harm to themselves.

My son was recently leafing through a toy catalog.

"Oh, cool! I want one of these," he said.

My wife looked at the toy and read the description out loud.

"Transforms your house into a fun-filled bowling alley," she intoned. "I don't think so."

What can you do?

If there are multiple children living under your roof, there is only one solution. Each room must be thoroughly soundproofed and only one activity that generates any type of sound may be carried out at any one time within any particular room. Sound impossible? It generally is. Enforcement of the noise ordinance is difficult, but if you don't, the city council will.

The next type of insulation is one that no one can help you with. I'm talking emotional protection here. As far as I know, the human race has yet to come up with something that will protect us from the unintentional verbal barbs from our own children. These are much easier to handle if you keep in mind that very young children really have no concept that what they do or say may be offensive. When it comes from your older children, however, it can have a tendency to be a bit more painful. But when your spouse starts in on you, you better pay attention!

I personally have developed the "duck" method for handling these verbal abuses. I just remember that people generally don't mean what they say when they are angry or upset and let the comments go "like water off the back of a duck." That way, when my youngest says, "I don't like you," I just reply with, "I think you're swell, too," and let it go. When he says, "Your breath stinks," I reply with a simple, "Thank you. I try."

I also call it the "duck" method as every now and then you have to dodge physical objects that come hurling through the air. These, however, are usually from the older children and not to be taken lightly as they have a more developed aim and a more powerful arm. That is why I have always reinforced in my children that they should "play fair" and never throw things at people when their backs are turned.

It is another matter, however, to protect the public at large. While in church one Sunday, my youngest announced to God and the entire congregation that the gentleman seated in front of us had no hair.

"That man has no hair!" he kept repeating in astute amazement and a steadily rising voice. While the man in front of us kindly pretended not to hear, most of the congregation certainly did. I would say that that man was either well insulated or totally deaf. Maybe he has kids. . . .

Another way to protect the people around you from the unpredictable antics of your children is to take two vehicles, if possible, whenever you dine out or go to special events. That way if something happens, one sacrificing adult can always remove the child who is having problems. This has come in handy on several occasions, like the time we were at a large, and lengthy, Christmas concert.

My youngest was getting bored, as music is not a great interest of his. He played quietly on the floor but eventually became distracted and was taking large gulps of water from his bottle to ease his boredom. Inevitably, some water went down the wrong way and he started choking. He quickly recovered, though, just in time for the audience's applause at the end of a song.

In the silence before the next piece started and to the amusement of those around us, he loudly announced, "Boy, I almost t'rew up!"

About then I decided the two of us had better call it a night. I calmly gathered him up and we headed out to the car.

"Why are we going?" he asked as I put on his coat.
"Because someone almost t'rew up!" I explained.
"Really?" he asked incredulously. "So did I!"
Sigh.

Then there is the final, but by no means trivial, case for

physical insulation. Just as you have to protect yourself from the sun or the cold, so you need to take certain precautions against your children. Just a few basic rules and articles of clothing are required to prevent great discomfort to your person.

Shoes: Any kind will do, except for open-toed shoes. The moment the shoes come off or the toes are exposed, your toes will get stepped on with a great probability that this will be perpetrated by the largest person in the room. My wife has this problem more than I do. She must simply keep her feet covered at all times. This rule is also important when walking down the street with your kids as they tend not to notice you if something catches their eye and are as likely to step on your heel as not. And heaven forbid you should trip! The whole family would walk right over you and never even realize it.

Shins: General protection should be taken if your kids are quick-tempered. This is generally where you get kicked if you should perchance deliver an unappreciated comment to your child. If you dare play soccer with your children, be warned. Use those shinguards!

Crotch: Most important when your children reach a certain height. Things that are thrown just naturally travel at that, um, certain level, if you know what I mean. Or if you roughhouse or wrestle with the kids, expect a foot to be kicked here. In fact, while we are at it, expect anything at any time. Men are just plain vulnerable and it doesn't take kids long to figure it out. Or spouses. Check out your local sports store for protective gear. Just tell them "kids" and they'll know what you are looking for.

Eyes: Safety goggles from your local hardware store can be an invaluable asset. This inexpensive item will keep sand, fingers, balls, and other foreign objects out of your eyes. You can get them in sporty tints, also. Tell your friends it's the latest in outdoor gear and they should get a pair. Then you won't look like the lone weirdo on the block.

Head: A full helmet would be great but I realize these tend to be heavy and hot. As a second option, bicycle helmets are currently the fashion rage, and they are designed to be cool and lightweight while giving you maximum protection from large sticks, rocks, and falls down the stairs.

The only problem with physical protection is that by the time you are ready to play catch with your kids, it is getting dark and you have so much gear on it looks like you are going out to play hockey or something. Now while the young boys in the family may say, "Cool, Dad," the girls are sure to run into the house and lock their doors.

"Dad, you are so embarrassing at times!"

Hey, you wanna play catch or not?

It seems you can never be too safe, these days. Accidents happen and modern society has devised all of these great aids to help secure the well-being of your physical self. My children know, however, that there is also the concept of safety of the spirit, of the mind and soul. There are just some things you don't even consider doing or saying because it puts you at risk and diminishes your self. You learn to avoid certain people and situations that put you in harm's way.

Contrary to popular belief, they don't make knee pads for the soul.

> *Lord, be with my family and keep us safe in Your spirit and love. Let us know what is good and decent in our hearts so that we always honor Your holy word, secure in knowing it is our protection and strength in this life.*

Dis-cuss-ions

*"Who despises a vile man but honors those who fear the
LORD, who keeps his oath even when it hurts."*
PSALM 15:4

Kids are natural mimics, so be careful, oh so very careful,
about what you say and do in their presence.

One evening when my middle daughter was around
three years old, we heard her apparently talking to herself in
her room. I peeked in to see what was going on, and she was
attempting to push the cat off her bed, saying, "Get off my
bed, Wuffie," followed by a few terms that we realized were
not normally accepted in polite society. Since that time we
have made a very conscious attempt to shelter our children
from the more colorful aspects of the English language.

Now, if there is one thing that is occasionally necessary
to do, it is to verbally vent your frustration. I don't mean
taking our Father's name in vain or resorting to vulgar
anatomical terminology. There is more than enough of this
in current society and I won't add to an already bad situation.
But there are some events that just require that extra bit of

emphasis that non-English terms can provide. I have found that it is most satisfying, and often somewhat entertaining, to make up your own "special" words. "Snazzlefrassin big-boppin frizzle-frazzle" is an oldie but goodie. I have also been known to turn in circles, roll my eyes back into their sockets, and just say, "Arrgh, arrgh!" until I feel better. Many times I just growl like a rabid dog. This is an especially effective release of pent-up frustration as it appeals to the more animal side of the male psyche. It also seems to be understood as a universal warning sign. When an animal growls at you, you back away and leave that animal alone, right? My kids even use this method now and then with various levels of success.

When we had company awhile back, my son had been asked to temporarily stifle his natural exuberance (in other words, be quiet). He sat down in the middle of the living room and commenced growling and grumbling, throwing in an occasional "poosies" for good measure.

"What is he doing?" asked our guest.

"Toddler-cussing," explained my wife.

Well, I guess it could be worse. We are constantly explaining to our children the definition of new words that they pick up at school. It is okay to know this stuff, we explain, but the use of it in our lives is something we try to discourage as much as possible. Kind of like knowing what poison ivy looks like so you can avoid touching it.

Remember the old Art Linkletter television show, *Kids Say the Darndest Things*? No? Well, if you can find the book in the library, it's worth the effort. Just keep in mind two things when you read it: One, if there is some way for a child to misuse a word or a pronunciation, they will. Two, if there can be an ultimately embarrassing time to say something about the family skeleton in the closet, they'll find it and say it. There isn't too much you can do about either case. Children just naturally misunderstand the events taking place around them, and even if you don't have any skeletons in your closet, the kids will make some up.

One day, one of my dear children came running up to me and announced, "I told my teacher on you!"

"Say what?" I asked.

"I told her you cheat on Mommy."

Oh, good grief!

"Fine," I moaned. "Just fine! Then tomorrow you can also tell her that you were referring to last night's Monopoly game. And I wasn't cheating, she was. She had five hundred dollars stuffed in her pocket!"

The improper use of words can be quite entertaining, also. Like when I went to pick up my son after preschool and there were a number of kids out front sliding across the new snow. "Look at me," boasted one young boy. "I'm telemarketing!" I'm sure he was referring to "telemarking," which is a style of skiing, as opposed to selling goods over the phone. But then again, maybe not. You never can be sure with today's kids.

Impressionables. Mimics. Sponges.

My kids do not particularly wish to be like their mother and father—unless it means they can do something which is usually verboten. Cleaning the house? Going to church? "Do I have to?" Staying up till midnight? "Can I stay up too?"

So, what do you do? Make sure they understand what is acceptable behavior and what is not. What words are okay and what aren't.

Sometimes just explaining what those words and terms really mean (in nitty-gritty detail), no matter how disgusting it may be, is the best cure against their use. The phrase "Knowledge is Power" can be your best weapon.

So ed-je-kate them chilluns!

> *Let me always remember, Lord, that I am never really alone, that there are always ears and eyes that hear and see everything I do. Help me as I try to be an example to those who watch me, and watch over me, so that my words do not condemn me.*

Emergencies and Angels

"Praise the LORD, you his angels,
you mighty ones who do his bidding,
who obey his word."
PSALM 103:20

There aren't very many things left that I haven't broken over the years. Besides countless glasses and a few windows, I have managed to fracture quite a few of the bones in my body, not to mention falls from high places and run-ins with large animals, siblings, barbed wire, and various sizes and forms of sticks and stones. I guess my family realized that country living had a few hazards associated with it and those were to be taken as a given and not to be worried about unless life-threatening. My parents probably would have been more concerned had they known the frequency or severity of some of my injuries, but I was reluctant to mention many of them due to the generally stupid nature in which most of them occurred.

I would prefer, however, that my children not have these experiences.

It is immensely frightening when you have to cart one of your children off to the hospital. These experiences, and those of my own dubious past, have led me to two conclusions. One is that the young usually heal quickly and the other is what I call the "hospital syndrome." This is the phenomenon wherein a child ill enough to be taken to the hospital will generally experience an almost miraculous recovery shortly after being admitted to the emergency room.

All of my children have been there and it always happens late at night or on a weekend. Their sudden fever is pushing 105 degrees. They lie listless and glassy-eyed in your arms as you overdose them with fever reducers and apply cool, wet washcloths to their foreheads. But nothing works. An hour or two later, you break down and warm up the car since this inevitably happens in the winter in the middle of a blizzard or the coldest weather in decades.

The emergency room is busy, of course, but that gives you time to fill out the forms, in triplicate, and promise to sell your possessions, if necessary, to pay for this visit while your spouse carries the sick little tyke back to the doctors. By the time you get back to see what is going on, your child is running around the place with a new teddy bear in his arms and maybe a temp of 100.5. The doctor says your child has a "virus" (never a cold or the flu or pneumonia or whatever is popular that week) and gives you a prescription for something new and fantastically expensive that won't work on viruses anyway. When you mention the 105 temp, the nurse looks at you like you have a second-grade education and offers to show you both how to read a thermometer. Those are awfully expensive teddy bears they give out at those hospitals.

But over the years, we have learned a few medical tricks. For instance, the gray color of the spots on the sides of the throat and the associated temperature determine the difference between the "sure thing" strep throat or the "maybe" strep throat, even though both are just as expensive at the doctor's office. At least we get the simple satisfaction of hearing the doctor say, "Yep, it's strep" or "Hmm. Might be strep," and having the diagnosis match our own.

Kids are tougher than we usually give them credit for, both emotionally and physically. This was driven home one day while we were skiing.

It had been my youngest daughter's first time on the ski slopes and she was doing great, good enough that we decided to have a go at the chairlift. My sister-in-law, the most experienced skier of us all, rode up with her, and my older daughter and I were five chairs back. We had almost gotten to the top when the chairlift suddenly slowed, then stopped. I couldn't see ahead to determine what the problem was. Then I heard some other skiers yelling, "Stop! Stop the lift! She's caught!"

I turned to my oldest daughter, fear and sickness rising up in my stomach. "It's your sister," was all I said.

After a fair amount of commotion and delay, the chairs started moving again. When ours crested the ridge, there stood my sister-in-law and daughter waiting for us.

I let out a big sigh of relief as we skied up to them.

"What was the problem?" I inquired.

My excited daughter filled me in on one revealing instant.

"Daddy, Daddy! I was flying!"

It had been her!

As I learned, my daughter had gone to get off the chairlift at the appropriate time. My sister-in-law was holding her hand to help her off. Neither one noticed that the belt to my daughter's coat had gotten caught in the chair. My sister-in-law first noticed something wrong when she looked down and saw that she was holding onto an abandoned ski mitten. She then looked up to see my daughter suspended a few feet under the chair hanging by her coat's waist belt and spinning like a top. The chair kept on going around the huge drive-wheel with my daughter calmly doing her best Peter Pan imitation. Just before she started to head back down the slope in this position, one of her skis tripped the emergency stop switch. The lift attendant was then able to help her get unstuck and re-joined with her very anxious aunt.

My daughter had enjoyed every moment. And she is still skiing, even though we no longer buy coats with belts or straps of any kind. And I now firmly believe that angels are real.

"Daddy, Daddy! I was flying!"

Let's talk about when angels are at their busiest, the time in every child's life when angels come out in swarms to ensure there will be a tomorrow. That time is kicked into high gear when your child is handed a piece of paper by a smiling woman who says, "Here is your learner's permit—drive carefully."

My daughter was doing surprisingly well. Her skills at keeping the car on the right side of the road were much improved. She only had one little problem—the infamous "right turn on red."

We approached the stop lights with great caution. She was the only one in the right lane as she was going to turn onto a busy street. The light was red. She slowed down.

"That's good, you're doing fine," my wife assured her.

But my daughter didn't stop.

She rounded the corner with a hint of squealing rubber. My wife stood on the nonexistent brake that is supposed to be on the passenger side of the car but had been omitted by some careless automobile designer.

The driver that my daughter had pulled out in front of did, however, apply his brakes. Hard. And his horn, as well. Hard.

The stream of adjectives applied to the situation by my wife was apparently impressive as my daughter recited a partial list later. Even I was impressed. Interspersed in the impromptu lecture was the fact that "right turn on red" meant you (first and foremost!) stopped and looked for oncoming traffic before proceeding. But it wasn't enough to break my daughter of her weakness. It helped but didn't cure.

Eventually my daughter passed her driver's test (they

must not have had the "right turn" question on the test) and seemed to be doing much better with this crucial maneuver—until the time she had a memory burp and repeated her prior error. While there was no actual contact of metal and plastic, it was close. Real close. This time, the other driver didn't just use her horn—the offended woman followed my daughter home and proceeded to loudly discuss the whys and wherefores of her turn in our driveway.

To my knowledge, my daughter has not committed this offense since. The woman who took the time to chew her out was obviously some form of an angel.

It was Christmas and we were newcomers in town. We hadn't had time to meet very many people and were feeling a little short on holiday spirit. When we saw the advertisement in the local paper that Santa Claus was going to be in town, we thought, why not, and took the kids to see the old guy.

We started to have second thoughts when we entered the abandoned little shop and were greeted by a woman whose outfit did not quite meet the Elfin dress code. She walked my youngest daughter over to the waiting Santa.

"Ho, ho!" he boomed in a jovial voice as he scooped her up onto his lap. "I know you, Elizabeth!"

He did? We sure didn't know him!

"Why, you just moved here from Nebraska, didn't you?"

"Uh-huh," my daughter confirmed as she tugged on his whiskers. He laughed at the expression on her face when she realized the beard was real.

"And you live in that pink house on North Street, don't you?"

"Uh-huh."

"And that is your sister, Katherine, over there, isn't it?" he asked cheerily.

"Yup."

Boy, this guy was good!

"And you are going to be three in the spring and you have two cats and your mom's name is Deb and your dad's name is Chris and they love you very much."

Who was this guy, anyway? And how did he know so much about us? It was uncanny.

"Well, tell me—what would you like for the Christ Mass, Elizabeth?"

I wondered at his terminology as my daughter thought about her reply.

"I don't know," she finally said.

"Well, here," he said as he fished a candy cane from the bag beside him. "How would you like a candy cane?"

My daughter paused before taking the treat from him.

"Not 'zactly what I had in mind," she mumbled.

Santa laughed and laughed and we knew he was for real. We never did find out who that guy was, but he sure brightened up the day for all of us. Must have been another one of those angels.

No matter how careful we try to be, accidents, illnesses, and just strange events happen. From what I've experienced, however, there are more angels out there watching over us than any of us can possibly imagine. Some of these angels may have very human faces, some we will never see with our eyes, only our hearts. But they are there, nonetheless. Take comfort in the thought that you, and your children, are never alone. Ever.

Lord of hosts, protect my family. This life is full of peril, but we know the rewards of the next life are great. Help me remember to seek Your presence in our daily lives. I know that You love us beyond measure, as a concerned parent for a beloved child.

The Mouths of Babes

"A time to tear and a time to mend,
a time to be silent and a time to speak."
ECCLESIASTES 3:7

It was time for the children's sermon, always a much-anticipated part of our church service. All the small children, including our two young girls, rushed up and sat in a semicircle around the pastor. His show-and-tells were infamous and this one would prove to be no different. He pulled a plain brown paper sack out from behind him. He slowly opened the sack. He pulled out a little stuffed bear.

I emitted an audible groan.

A month ago, I had cleaned out the kids' overflowing toy box. The abandoned or forgotten toys had somehow magically reappeared in the church nursery. And now at the pulpit.

"Hey!" piped my young daughter. She had yet to learn how to control her vocal volume and could be plainly heard throughout the church.

"Hey!" she said again. "I have a bear just like that!" She looked closer. "Hey! That is my bear! How'd you get my bear? Did you find him or somethin'? I've been lookin' for that bear."

Our pastor was visibly taken aback.

"Well, uh, I. . ."

"Maybe he just wanted to come to church," my daughter continued among chuckles from the congregation. I slunk down in the pew. "Or maybe he was just lost an' now we've found him."

"I rest my case," said the clergyman as he handed the bear back to my daughter. The audience applauded loudly as my older daughter glanced nervously at her younger sister. "Maybe we should just skip to exhibit number two." He pulled an empty glass mason jar from the sack. Now that was not now, nor had it ever been, ours.

"Does everyone know what this is?" he asked.

"It's a jar," the children dutifully echoed.

"Can you think of something that we put in jars?" asked the pastor innocently.

There was a moment of silence as the children thought. Just a moment. Then the same shrill little voice piped up once again.

"We mostly just put bugs in our jars," she stated. Her sister, sitting next to her, visibly wilted.

"Well, yes," our pastor agreed. I could see he had paled a bit. "Anyone else?"

No one had a chance as my daughter took off on a verbal barrage.

"An' we go an' catch fireflies an' my dad puts them in the jar an' they glow an' they make a great night-light 'cause they're so bright when they blink an' all. . . ."

The pastor's mouth hung open and my older daughter nudged her sibling in the ribs.

"An' we lets them out in the morning, but my sister doesn't like to touch them, so I have to catch them all when it starts to get dark." The little kid paused to come up for air. Several people in the congregation gasped as they realized her obvious lung capacity. Everyone, including the other children, were mesmerized by her performance—except her sister, who was trying unsuccessfully to hold her down with one arm and cover her mouth with the other. My daughter's voice rose half an octave as she fought off her older sibling.

"An' in the daytime we likes to catch butterflies but my dad makes us let them go 'cause they're for everyone an' if the cat gets them, he eats them, but he likes bunnies ever so much better so we have to take them away from him except sometimes he eats them an'. . . ." She took another breath while fending off her older sister's efforts to subdue her. ". . .then they're dead an' everything."

My older daughter finally got her hand over the little mouth. The Talker struggled a moment before breaking free and stating, "Well, he asked!"

The congregation roared and the spell was broken. The minister hurriedly finished his sermon, albeit a much abbreviated version.

Everyone enjoyed the performance save the older sister. Mother and Father were slightly embarrassed by the timing of the speech, but we had laughed as hard as anyone. It could have been worse.

Freedom of speech is a big thing in this country. It is a basic right we have all enjoyed immensely. Children have a basic need to express themselves as well, in whatever manner they are capable. Enjoy it when you can, for the day will come when you get unintelligible grunts and groans in response to your well-meaning queries. I guess that's one reason we really like to gather together at least once a day, usually at the dinner table, for food and conversation. Everyone understands it is the opportunity for a more or less open forum and a chance to catch up on what is happening in our children's lives. Within reason, of course. We try to limit the shouting and any open hostilities that may arise. And parent bashing is strictly limited to the second Friday of every other month.

I pray my children will always be willing to communicate, dear Lord, so that we will know of their fears and concerns, joys and hopes. Help us teach them what is appropriate so that when they speak, their words will be full of grace, seasoned with the salt of Your holy word, and that they will always know what to say, and when.

Volume Control

"Shout for joy to the LORD,
all the earth.
Worship the LORD with gladness;
come before him with joyful songs."
PSALM 100:1–2

Let's face the truth here. Children do not come with a built-in volume control. Never have, never will. If things ever get a little noisy at work, all I have to do is come home to realize just how peaceful it really is there. The decibel barrage starts when I sneakily ease open the front door. You have to be careful because you never can tell what to expect when you walk in the house, or what role you will be playing a moment later.

"Dad's home!"

"Hi, Dad!"

I have been recognized to exist! How nice. And then it starts.

"Hey, Dad, have you seen my. . . ?"

"I need some new tennis shoes. Can you take me to. . . ?"

This is what I call the Servant mode. Still, it is nice to be needed. Sometimes.

"She hit me!"

"Well, he. . ."

"Did not!"

Referee mode. Keep the peace at any cost.

"Can I have my allowance?"

"I need lunch money."

"Can we get. . . ?"

Financier mode. Shovel out the cash.

"The toilet is plugged with. . ."

"The computer isn't working right and I need to. . ."

"Dad, my bicycle broke. Can you. . . ?"

Repairman mode. Get out the superglue.

"Can you help me with my science project?"

"Who was the first person to. . . ?"

"Why do porcupines. . . ?"

Educator mode. Lie through your teeth.

I should be grateful. At least they still speak to me.

Similarly, supper is always an interesting time. We all sit down at the table and have the one chance to really be heard by everyone and receive a little attention. Unfortunately, it too often turns out to be the wrong kind of attention as everyone tries to be heard at the same time.

"At school today I—"

"But you should have seen them—"

"Please pass—"

"I don't feel very—"

"Is there salt on the table?"

"Then our teacher made us—"

Now, during most of these enlightening exchanges, I spend my time shoveling food into my mouth and listening to as many of the sound bites as I can and I try to make some sense out of it all. Occasionally, I add a "Hmm" or "Uh-huh," but mostly I stuff my face and listen.

"Then the school had to be evacuated. . . ."

Hmm.

"I think I ate my marble. . . ."

Uh-huh.

"And I had to punch Jimmy so hard he. . ."

That's nice.

All the time, the volume is creeping up as each child tries to be heard above his or her siblings. Doing this for extended periods of time can lead to the habit of always shouting to be heard, even when you are talking to yourself.

The phone was ringing in the background. It does that more and more as your children migrate toward and through the teenage years.

"You can't talk now—we're eating!" I reminded my daughter.

"But it's. . ."

"Has anyone seen the salt?"

"I tink I'm gonna t'row up."

". . .for you."

I take the phone. "Hello," I bark.

"Uh, good evening, sir. I'm calling to. . ."

"Dad! He's gonna hurl!"

". . .credit card with low annual. . ."

"Don't do it!" I snap to no one in particular.

"Children! Quiet!" calmly interjected my wife. Sudden silence.

Man, I wish I could do that.

"Look, miss. This isn't really a convenient time to talk right now. Why don't you give me your home phone number and I'll call you back when things slow down a bit—say around two in the morning?"

"Well, I, uh. . ."

"Okay, thanks for thinking of us. Bye now." I hung up the phone.

After the evening meal, we like to relax a little. This generally involves listening to various musical artists simultaneously wailing on the stereo with a television show thrown in for the fun of it. Sometimes this pastime is joined by music practice, which in our house could be French horn, oboe, bassoon, piano, flute, drums, etcetera. Usually my youngest enjoys chasing around the house doing respectable imitations of, say, an automobile wreck on his tricycle or a reenactment of the gunfight at the OK Corral. Needless to say, things sometimes get a little out of control.

When, at last, everyone is in bed and asleep, I like to roam around the house and savor the quiet. The difference an hour can make is almost eerie and reminds me of walking through a church on a weekday. Reverent. Peaceful. I know it will not last. Come morning, it will start all over again. Thank God.

I thank You for the sounds of life in our household, Lord. I thank You that my children are healthy enough to want to make noise and be active and have the opportunity of youth. Help me remember my own youth and not begrudge my children the joyful, noisy experience of childhood.

Good Morning

*"The LORD himself goes before you
and will be with you;
he will never leave you nor forsake you.
Do not be afraid; do not be discouraged."*
DEUTERONOMY 31:8

I dread mornings. Around our house, every day starts off with a challenge of some kind or another. Things aren't so bad in the summer when I have to be at work earlier, but the other nine months age me considerably. They say that men are most likely to have heart attacks in the morning. I believe it.

Brrr-ring!

Oh, joy. Morning. I heard the shower running and knew my wife had, as usual, usurped the bathroom for the next few minutes. I bonked the alarm for a little more snooze time.

"Daddy, I can't find my little barking dog," pleaded a little voice in my ear.

Who needs an alarm when there are young children in the house?

"Uh huh. Look under your bed."

Then I decided I might as well get on with Morning Phase One and slowly rolled out of bed and headed upstairs to make some double-strength coffee, running my hand through what little hair I had left to smooth down the Kewpie-doll peak that magically appears every morning at about this time.

"Is anyone down here with me?" I heard my son yell with a hint of panic in his voice. He doesn't like to be left alone downstairs. Or upstairs either, for that matter. Let's face it—he doesn't like to be alone.

"Mom is down there," I yelled back, nervously eyeing the cat as he impatiently sat next to his empty food bowl. He looked up at me and meowed.

"Yeah, yeah. Later," I told him.

Satisfied that the coffee was brewing, I headed back down.

The cat pounced on my right foot and bit me. I shook my foot violently to free myself from the carnivore.

"Sheesh, cat! Not very patient this morning, are we? Well, you're gonna have to wait until I wake up. Priorities."

Halfway through my shower, the bathroom door burst open.

"I can't find my barking dog," my son repeated.

"Look in your toy box," I shouted over the shower. The shower door opened, revealing my son clutching his blanket.

"What?"

"I said, look in your toy box."

"I did."

"Did you look upstairs?" I asked as shampoo ran down into my eyes.

"Huh?"

I guess I needed to be more specific. "Did you look for your dog in the living room? Under the coffee table maybe."

"No one is upstairs."

Sigh. "Wait a few minutes and I'll go up with you."

Silence.

I shut the door. It opened up again. He was still standing there. Kinda gave me the creeps.

"Yes?"

"What are you doing?"

"What does it look like I'm doing?"

"Taking a shower?"

"Bingo. Now let me finish, please." I shut the door again. A moment later it opened back up.

"Daddy?"

I was getting exasperated. "Yes?"

In typical childlike fashion, he shared an observation with me about certain anatomical parts of the male body.

"Thank you for noticing. May I finish my shower now?"

"When I grow up, will I have—?"

"The question is, *if* you grow up. Now scram!"

I hurriedly finished before there were any more interruptions, wrapped a towel around me, and headed upstairs for the coffee. I poured a cup for my wife and one for myself and started back down with a cup in each hand when the cat pounced on my foot again.

"Yeow! Get off me!" I yelled, shaking my foot and spilling hot coffee on my arm. "Ee-yaaah!" The cat gave up and wandered over to his food bowl, sulking and plotting his next attack.

As I handed my spouse her coffee, I mentioned that mornings were not in my job description. She casually pulled out a piece of paper from under her dressing table and simply said, "Section B, Paragraph Four."

"Funny. Very funny."

I would have debated the issue with her, but it was time to start Morning Phase Two.

"By the way, your foot is bleeding."

"Cat."

She nodded with understanding.

I hurriedly got dressed and carried the little Peeping Tom, blankie and all, upstairs and set him down at the kitchen table. I then dug out every cereal box in the cupboard, a bowl, spoon, and carton of milk and set them in front of him. Then, while he was making up his mind as to which sugar-fortified, artificially enhanced item to start with, I went to wake up his sisters.

"Time to get up," I sang out cheerily. No response from one room and a sleepy plea for five more minutes from the other. I glanced at my watch. Okay, five minutes.

Back to the kitchen, where I dug out the cat food as the starving animal brushed back and forth against my legs. Oh, sure, now be affectionate. But I must have been too slow, for he suddenly bit my foot one last time and then quickly let go when I sat the bowl on the floor. What a psycho animal! Good thing he doesn't have very many teeth.

"Daaad. I spilled."

Without even looking as to the extent of the spill, I grabbed a dishcloth. When I got to the table, milk was dripping through the leaf-cracks. I mopped quickly, poured milk from the overflowing bowl back into the carton, cereal and all, and then went back to the girls.

"Time to get up," I announced again. "Now!"

"Five more minutes!"

"Now!"

Back to the kitchen, where I picked spilled cereal off the floor and put it into my son's overflowing bowl.

"Having problems?" I commented.

He looked at me and just grinned.

Ten minutes later, the place was in a hubbub of complaints and conversation as the girls joined us and started wolfing down whatever they could find to eat. They knew that, being older, they were on their own for breakfast.

"Why are there soggy pieces of cereal in the milk carton?"

"And then I told Mary Ann. . ."

"The cat wants out."

"I need lunch money."

"But the teacher wouldn't. . ."

"Where is my barking dog?"

"Is Mom up yet? I need her to. . ."

Overload! Warning! Danger, Will Robinson! Aliens attacking!

I just mumbled, "Uh-huh," and put dirty dishes into

the dishwasher. I glanced out the window and noticed a garbage can along the street. Oh no! Garbage day. I grabbed a garbage sack and proceeded to rush around the house frantically emptying overflowing garbage cans. I then rushed out into the freezing wind, dumped the bulging sacks on the curb, and heard the far-off rumble of the garbage truck.

Whew! Made it.

Then I glanced at my watch. Holy cow! If we don't leave now, the kids will be late for school and I won't be able to find a place to park at work. I rushed back into the house.

"Everyone ready to go?"

I noticed my son was dressed, courtesy of my wife. My older daughter was waiting at the door, ready to go.

"Where is your sister?" I asked.

She shrugged her shoulders as I tossed her the car keys.

"Start her up!" I yelled to her and she shot out the door. She likes starting the car. Gives her a sense of power.

"We're running late," I yelled to the other daughter as I struggled to get my son's shoes on and teeth brushed.

I grabbed my own coat and handed my daughter her lunch money.

"Oh, no!" she moaned. "I forgot to tell you that there's no hot lunch today!"

"Aaaaah!" I yelled as I ran back to the kitchen. I felt I was either going to go ballistic or climb in the sink and cry. Instead, I pulled myself together by repeating just under my breath, "You can do this, you can do this." I opened the refrigerator and threw whatever small, loose items I could find into a lunch sack. Plain yogurt, moldy cheese slices, green bologna. That'll teach her to pull last-minute surprises on her old man.

I went tearing down the steps where my son was vainly struggling to get his coat on. I saw through the window that both girls were sitting in the car. You'd think they could have helped their brother with his coat, but noooo! I scooped him up and carried him under my arm out to the car so I wouldn't blow a cork waiting for him to come along and, for the ten thousandth time, watched as he tried to get in the "wrong" side of the car (his sisters having taken their traditional seats on that side of the vehicle).

"Hey! My barking dog!" He picked the toy off the floor of the car.

Then we were off on Morning Phase Three, and the daily argument on whose turn it was to walk their brother into school started between the girls. Not that either one of them wanted to, you see. And as usual, I could not remember who had done it the day before, so I had to arbitrarily choose one, much to the other's delight. In the background, the radio blared, the barking dog barked. I handed the sack lunch to my daughter.

"Don't call me if you get sick," I warned.

A few minutes later, we pulled up to the school and I waited impatiently as, as usual, the girls got out and left their brother strapped in the backseat, struggling to free himself. I leaned back and extracted him from the seat belt, and the last I saw, he was running after his older siblings.

Peace at last!

Then I remembered that I had neglected to pack myself a lunch. I glanced at my watch. Well, too late now—if I wasn't at work in the next five minutes, all the parking places would be gone. I went to put the car in gear and my hand brushed a forgotten lunch sack.

Sigh.

For a moment I considered absconding with it. I dutifully carried it into school and my daughter instead.

Well, it had been a good try. Maybe tomorrow. . . .

Over the years, I have gotten the reputation for being a hard worker and getting things done. The people I work with understand that I am a little strange, however, and put up with my idiosyncrasies. They casually try not to stare at me when I talk to myself and slowly back away when I stomp down the hall growling. Someone once asked me how I deal with the madhouse that is my work. I pulled open my desk drawer and tossed him one of those buttons with smart aleck sayings on it.

It said, "I can handle anything—I have kids."

Please give me the strength, Lord, to see me through this day. Help me be calm in the face of chaos, to be a pillar when the storm rages around me. My children need this from me, dear Lord, but I can't do it without You.

Travelogue

"Again, it will be like a man going on a journey,
who called his servants and
entrusted his property to them."
MATTHEW 25:14

Extended travel (those periods over five minutes in length) with children can be trying, to say the least. Seating arrangements, travel necessities, and general boredom can all be problems that parents must deal with while navigating strange roads and unexpected driving conditions. I have also discovered that the larger the vehicle, the better, for this allows each person traveling with you to have some semblance of his or her own private space. But even with the modern convenience of a minivan, nothing can really help on a long trip when children are involved.

"Okay, everyone have all their stuff?" I asked as we got into the car, looking around and mentally ticking off all the necessities: water jug, car snacks, wet washcloth, music tapes, pillows, suitcases, car toys, camera.

"I think we're set," replied my wife.

"I can't see," said my son.

"Do I have to sit next to him?" asked my daughter.

I looked in the rearview mirror as I started up the car and something caught my eye. My youngest daughter, who was unusually quiet, was looking slightly nervous. Then I saw her shirt pocket move.

"Hey, Miss Sneak. The mouse stays home."

"Aw, Dad! He won't hurt anything."

"Home."

She reluctantly climbed out and disappeared into the house.

I started the engine.

"I have to go to the bathroom," said my son.

Never fails.

I unbuckled him and hustled him into the bathroom and took advantage of the time to make a quick check of the house, turning off lights, radios, and the coffee pot. Then I rounded up my son, locked the door behind us, and we climbed back into the car.

"We're off," I sighed as I backed out of the drive.

"I think not," argued my wife.

"No?"

"No."

"Why?"

About then my daughter burst from the house and came running toward us.

"Oh."

"I didn't know we were leaving right now," she panted as she climbed in the van.

"You thought maybe we were just sitting in the car for the fun of it?" I asked.

Okay. I looked back and counted. Five bodies in all. Ready to roll.

We almost reached the outskirts of town and I knew what was coming. I already had my blinker on and was in the process of turning into Burger Joint when I heard the familiar chorus of "I'm hungry." Do I know my family, or what?! As usual, I reminded the kids that no honey, mustard, or ketchup was allowed in the car, so order accordingly.

After we had gotten the food situation taken care of and once again started on our way, things quieted considerably as the kids proceeded to chow down. I waited patiently for the next comment. Sure enough, about ten minutes later, my son said, "My tummy hurts."

"You'll feel better in a few minutes," my wife reassured him.

"Can I take off my seat belt now?"

"No," asserted my spouse and myself at the same time. She shot a troubled look in my direction.

There is this phenomenon that people who have been together a long time develop. They both say things or answer questions in unison, almost like they have become telepathic in some weird way or are starting to think alike. I know this bothers my wife immensely—the prospect of thinking like me gives her the willies.

"Oh, look!" I exclaimed as I tried to take my son's mind off of his ailing innards. "Antelope!"

"Where?"

"Look out the window."

"Where?"

"On your right."

"Where?"

"Your other right," my wife and I said in unison. She rolled her eyes and looked out the window.

"I don't see any antelope."

"Too late. They're gone now."

"Where'd they go?"

Arrgh!

"Behind us about a mile."

"What?"

Then the other kids started to get restless.

"How much longer until we get there?"

"About two hours."

"What?"

"About two hours," I repeated louder, forgetting how kids' hearing deteriorates in the close quarters of an automobile.

"Oh."

Five minutes later, I heard the question repeated. Kids have a very poor sense of time, especially when riding in a car. It's as if time is suspended once the engine starts. Minutes stretch into eternity. Want to live longer? Just go on a lot of car trips. But then again, the stress of all that traveling with your family will probably cut your life span in half.

I returned to the question at hand.

"About five minutes less than the last time you asked."

"Oh."

Silence.

Things progressed well for a few miles. Then a scuffle started.

"Dad! He won't stop kicking the seat."

"Stop kicking the seat," I reaffirmed.

"But she's sitting on my blanket."

"So you have to kick the seat?" And then to the offending daughter I said, "Don't sit on his blanket."

"I'm not."

Of course I couldn't see low enough in the rearview mirror to determine what exactly was going on in back, so I took the neutral stand.

"Then both of you stop it!"

I glanced back again to see my oldest daughter in the far back, grinning as she slowly pulled my son's blanket over the seat without him noticing.

"Put it back!" I warned.

Her smile faded as she returned the coveted blanket to her brother.

"How much longer until we get there?"

"Stop asking!" my wife and I replied at the same time.

Then my beloved groaned, turned to me, and hissed, "Stop it."

"No, you stop it."

"Both of you stop it," warned my son, "or you'll be sorry." He shook his little fist at us.

A rest stop sign loomed up ahead.

"Anyone have to go to the bathroom?" I asked.

No response.

"Last chance for an hour."

Still no response.

"Pull over anyway," my wife said.

After we had stopped, the girls trudged into the rest room with their mom.

"Sure you don't need to go?" I asked the little guy.

"Go where?"

"To the bathroom."

"No."

"Want to do a few laps around the building?"

"No."

The others came back. We started off.

We almost made it to the highway when my son said, "I have to go potty."

Fine. I made a U-turn back to the rest area. Better now than alongside the highway.

Finally we were off again.

"How much longer now?" Now they were doing it just to annoy me.

Grrr. It was working.

"Still about an hour."

Giggles from the back. My wife glanced back to see the blanket creeping over the back of the seat and was forced to use her ultimate car threat.

"Don't make me come back there," she warned. The blanket slowly crept back beside my oblivious son.

She then turned to me. "I just had a great idea," she whispered with a smile. "Next time we have to go any-where with the kids, I'll. . ."

"Just stay at home?" I finished for her.

"Stop it!"

After all these years, you'd think I would learn when to keep my mouth shut. Next week the kids and I are going to visit my folks. Less wife.

I think I'll get one of those portable TV sets for the backseat.

We had to stop for gas or we would be sore pressed to make our destination. I pulled into a likely looking service station and turned off the car.

"Anyone need anything?" I innocently asked.

Immediately I was besieged by a plethora of orders for pop, gum, chips, and other nourishing edibles.

Except from my son, who was looking back and forth nervously. I could tell what was coming.

"Are you getting gas?" he asked.

I could not lie.

"Yes, but I'm sure it'll go away with a good antacid," I joked.

"Noooo," he wailed. "No gas. No no no!"

The girls groaned.

I don't know how or exactly when, but he had somehow developed a dreaded case of petrol-phobia.

"It's okay," I assured him. "The car has to have gas to go. It won't hurt you."

"Nope. Uh-uh. No gas," he repeated. His eyes welled up with tears.

My wife shook her head at the frightened little kid's vocalizations.

"Why don't you have him help you fill up the car," she suggested.

The kid suddenly stopped his tirade.

"You mean I can help?"

"Sure," I said.

And he did.

Now he wants to help fill up every time we stop, whether we need to or not. Go figure!

When we were going for a bike ride one evening, my son's friend, who was not allowed to journey more than a few houses in any direction of his own, wanted to come along. After securing permission from his parents, we set off down the street. As we rounded the first corner, the innocent exclaimed, "Wow! It's a whole new world!"

So it is with us all. Just around the corner lies a whole new world, one of infinite beauty and joy and wonder. Sometimes we need a little help along the way, and we shouldn't be afraid or embarrassed to ask for directions. Sometimes the simplest of actions can make it so much easier.

Let us journey together.

Lord God, keep us safe on the sometimes long and dangerous journeys in this life. Protect and strengthen us through Your grace and love as You guide us to our intended destination.

True Love

*"You are my friends if
you do what I command."*
JOHN 15:14

We all worry about our children. If you love them, it is just natural that you are concerned for their safety and well-being. We worry when they are ill, when they are sad, when the world they will inherit seems to be going steadily down the toilet like so many dead fish. Most of the time, these periods of concern are brief and unwarranted. Other times they are not. It helps relieve some of my fears, however, to think back to when I was a kid and remember the wanton pollution, chemicals in everything, medical care, threat of nuclear holocaust, and the cold war, and then things don't seem to be quite so bad. On the other hand, today's society has its own unique set of problems that we, and our children, must deal with.

As I have told my children, to worry about someone is another way of saying "I love you." So, how do I love you? Let me count the ways. . . .

I love you enough to make you wear your bike helmet.

When my eldest daughter was little, they didn't have such things as bicycle helmets. This led to her learning some new words at an early age, words like "CAT scan" and "concussion." But even when she was much older and it was "cool" to wear aerodynamic, state-of-the-art, big-bucks headgear, there were times when she still didn't want to wear her helmet.

"I'm just fooling around in front of the house," she said one day. "Why do I have to wear my helmet?"

I gave her the standard reply.

"Because I said so."

"Aw, Dad."

"Look, remember the story about what happened to me when I was a little kid, right before we moved to the ranch?"

She sighed and eyed the neighborhood kids riding aimlessly around in the street. "Yeah, yeah. A car came over a hill at about a zillion miles an hour and landed on top of you and the last things you remembered until the police picked you off of some yard was flying like Peter Pan and the lady next door screaming her head off."

"Well, there you go."

"Dad, we live on the end of a dead-end street and there are no hills on it."

I bent over to one side, curled up my arm, rolled my eyes, and let my tongue hang out the corner of my mouth. A natural pose, I thought.

"You want to end up like me?" I asked.

"Dad! You're embarrassing me!"

Sometimes timing and fortune are on your side. Sometimes.

Immediately after I straightened up, we both happened to look over at the other kids riding around and yelling at each other, when one younger boy turned too sharply and his bike came to a screeching stop, but he didn't. In an instant he found himself up close and personal with the asphalt street. He had on his helmet, however, and was able to slowly get back up after his ears stopped ringing. He immediately started kicking and beating on his bike (sometimes you have to do that to your bike to keep it in its place).

My daughter turned to me, mouth hanging open, and said, "Oh. I see."

End of discussion. She put on her helmet.

Meanwhile, the smaller children in the crowd had suddenly decided to be helpful and joined the angry little boy in reprimanding his bicycle.

It turned out to be ugly. Very ugly. I'm not sure, but I think the bike died.

I love you enough not to let you pig out on candy.

It was a week after his birthday and my son had left a trail of chocolate fingerprints on the wall leading into the bathroom. Yes! Now I knew where his stash was! My daughters, being older, always had their candy stashes well hidden, but this little guy hadn't yet discovered what Dad was like when he was around chocolate. But he was beginning to suspect.

I carefully tested the bathroom door.

Locked! Looked like I had to switch to a different strategy.

"This is the candy police," I gruffly yelled from outside the bathroom door. "Put down the candy and come out with your hands up. I repeat, put down the candy!"

From inside the bathroom, I heard complete silence and then a little voice piped up.

"Is this really the police?"

"Sure is, son. Now come along quietly and things will go easier for you."

"The candy police! Cool!"

Are my kids gullible, or what!?

The doorknob started to turn.

Unfortunately, my daughter's room is just around the corner. Normally these kids fight like cats and dogs. Give them an opportunity to side against an adult, however, and they are suddenly the best of buddies and seek every possible chance to help each other out.

"Don't open the door! It's Dad! He wants your candy!"

What a spoilsport.

I made a futile grab for her and she slammed her door in my face.

I gave up and wandered back to my book. Sometimes you win a few and sometimes you don't. Or in my case, sometimes you lose the vast majority.

I love you enough to support your decisions.

We have always tried to instill as much self-reliance as

possible in our children. We taught them to be polite. We gave them responsibility. We showed them the difference between right and wrong. We told them not to let themselves be taken advantage of. You take responsibility for your own actions, we said, but if you do the right thing and still get into trouble, we'll back you up. We told the girls they were not to be treated any differently from anyone else and to take pride in the fact that they were females and not, as some women are quick to describe us males, "hormonally rampant creatures from outer space."

Ouch.

But I am really a pacifist. Violence is not my thing at all. Still, we have given our children a certain amount of advice and instruction on basic self-defense techniques. Never hurts.

Then, one day, I got that inevitable call from my younger daughter's teacher.

"Mr. Ewing?" she asked.

"Maybe."

"I just want to verify something your daughter said."

"Yeeesss?" I cautiously responded.

"Well, I'm afraid there has been a bit of a misunderstanding and a little bit of trouble. Did you tell your daughter she could kick boys in the crotch?"

Oooo. Let's get right to the point, shall we? And did I tell her? Hmph, I taught her! But we also had imposed certain restrictions on the use of this type of deadly force—including never use it on their father.

"Well, yes," I stammered, "as long as it was in self-defense. What happened?"

"It seems that one of the boys had been teasing your daughter and she got quite upset and, well, she just sort of snapped. But I'm sure the young man will be okay."

Too bad, I thought.

"I don't think your daughter seems to realize," the teacher continued, "that this is not the way we resolve conflicts."

Believe me, I have been in some situations with kids who were so totally psycho that this type of reasoning was the only way to resolve conflicts and the only language they understood. And if this was the kid that she said had been bugging her lately, the shoe fit.

I struggled to keep my voice from cracking with laughter as, in my best pseudopsychologist manner, I apologized for my daughter's behavior.

"I'm sorry about this unfortunate incident. I will personally have a little talk with my daughter about the appropriateness of her actions and suggest some alternative methods of conflict resolution."

Yeah. Like how to put a choke hold on the little creeps!

Still, that evening, I reluctantly explained under what circumstances it was appropriate to use physical violence and when it was better to just walk away. But from hearing her side of the story, it was just as I had suspected earlier, and I really couldn't be too upset with her. At least she had gotten the kid's attention and her point was taken seriously.

He never bothered her again.

Love comes in many unique flavors, many varied and subtle hues. You show love by protecting your children as much as possible, by allowing them a certain amount of freedom, and by supporting them, whenever possible, in their decisions. You show them love by giving them a comfortable home and teaching them right from wrong. They, in turn, show you love by not doing irreparable harm to your person or psyche.

It's an even trade.

Forgive me, Father, for not showing or telling those people I love how much I care for them as often as I should. They know I love them and I know they love me. But sometimes this doesn't seem like enough. Help me to remember Your great sacrifice for us and open my heart to my children and to You.

Child Prodigies

"The father of a righteous man
has great joy;
he who has a wise son
delights in him."
PROVERBS 23:24

Everyone has a talent. It may be anything from concert pianist abilities to painting beautiful landscapes to having the knack for fixing things. These gifts usually make themselves known at an early age and should be actively encouraged by parents. My daughters seem to take after their mother and are blessed with music and artistic abilities that I have come to cherish. I even have a talent—I can hang a spoon off the end of my nose.

My son's talent, however, has not yet fully shown itself, unless getting into trouble counts.

"Say, isn't that my screwdriver?" I inquired as he came walking up the stairs, sharp tool clutched in a dirty little hand.

"NO," he snapped. "It's mine!"

"Oh. Excuse me. It looked just like one of mine."

"It's my 'crewdriver." (He has a little trouble with that "sc" combination.)

"I see. I thought you had plastic ones. You know, bright colors, red, green, yellow. . ."

"This one works better."

Suspicion edged into my mind.

"You haven't been poking anything or anyone with that, have you?"

He looked at me with a blank expression on his face.

"Good. Don't. And just what have you been doing for the last fifteen minutes, anyway?"

"Working."

"Been working hard?"

The little truant beamed me a big smile and proudly announced, "I fixed the door."

Uh, oh. Better check this out, I thought. I went down to our front door, which, upon a cursory inspection, looked normal enough. No gouges or holes at least. Then my wife called us all to dinner and immediately the door check was gone from my mind as I bounded up the stairs to the kitchen. I noticed Mr. Mechanic no longer had the weapon of choice, and I made a mental note to find the screwdriver at the first opportunity and put it safely back in my "den," a.k.a. the garage.

Halfway through supper, the doorbell rang (that being the normal time for doorbells and telephones to ring). All the kids made a tentative motion to jump up and see who was calling on us, but I quickly thwarted the curious attempt with a single "SIT!" I smiled as they all grudgingly plopped back into their chairs and silently wished I could train the dog like that. I trudged to the door and saw my two favorite neighborhood merchants out front. Then I saw the Girl Scout cookie order forms clutched in their hands.

I love Girl Scout cookies.

I grabbed the door handle and pulled.

Now I suppose that the look on my face through the door's window as the handle came off in my hand must have been reasonably humorous because those girls got this surprised look on their faces and then burst into sidesplitting laughter. Perhaps their reaction was due to the outside doorknob falling on the ground and rolling to their feet. Or maybe it was the slow motion of the big door falling inward on top of me, pulling the top hinge out of the wall as it fell. I'll never know, because by the time I had caught the door, gotten it propped up against the wall, and stopped my colorful stream of adjectives, they were gone.

Man! I sure would have liked to have ordered some of those cookies.

But what really bothers me is that I have yet to find that screwdriver, and a curtain-pull holder-doohicky fell off the wall yesterday. The screws that held it to the wall were mysteriously gone.

And now my hammer seems to be missing, also.

Now, my middle child has developed a talent that is rather unique. While we enjoy showing it off on rare occasion, that doesn't necessarily mean we condone or encourage it either, and have expressed these same sentiments to our daughter.

You see, she swallows air.

Swallows air? How special can that be, you ask? As well you may. As did her grandmother on a recent visit.

My daughter stood proudly in the middle of the living room, family gathered around to witness this singular talent. She made little fish motions with her mouth—open, close, open, close, open, close, open. Then the coup de grace.

"Bbrrrraaaaaaaaaapppphh!"

A wonderful belch! About twelve seconds and a good seventy decibels. I could tell by the wide-eyed expression on my mother-in-law's face and her stunned silence that even she was genuinely impressed. The rest of the family burst out into shocked laughter and laughed until they cried. Who could ask for better entertainment?!

Hmm. Maybe there was some money in this somewhere. Commercials, maybe.

"Do it again, honey," I urged.

My wife glared at me with that look that says, "Not!"

"Well, she has to practice piano, doesn't she?"

"This is not the piano!"

"Well, maybe she could learn to burp in tune to 'The Star Spangled Banner' or something? And I saw *Ben Hur* last night and there was belching in that movie. Maybe she could burp for all the big names in Hollywood someday!"

My wife planted a kidney punch to the small of my back.

"Okay, okay!" I painfully conceded.

Sometimes you have to know when to let a great idea go, or else it hurts. I mean, no matter how much it hurts.

There was no doubt I was in for it when we attended a church function. We had to sign in at a front table and our four-year-old insisted on signing her own name. She carefully wrote her name for the woman, a teacher in real life, who sat behind the table. I looked at the writing but could not recognize it for any language I knew of.

"Dyslexic?" I asked.

The woman smiled and said, "Oh, I don't think it's anything to worry. . ." Her voice trailed off and the smile slowly faded from her face.

"What?" my wife asked, suddenly worried.

The woman turned the page so we could see the scrawls. My daughter's full name jumped out at us, perfectly written. However, she had written it backwards and upside down, from our viewpoint, so it would appear correct to the woman across the desk as she wrote it.

I tried it. My wife tried it. We could not duplicate the feat.

I couldn't get the *Twilight Zone* theme song out of my head for days.

Every child among us has a talent and purpose, no matter how seemingly insignificant or obscure in nature. As parents and people of God, we have a huge obligation to direct and nurture those strengths and talents to the betterment of the human race. What a horrible waste to stifle creativeness, what a wonderful blessing to use our intelligence to serve the world. These gifts start with us and, through our children and their actions, will lead us to a better tomorrow for all. And sometimes that gift is to simply be loved by others.

Bless my children, Lord, with gifts that glorify You and bring joy to others. Help me gently guide my children as they come to know their place in Your world. Help me to remember that we all have gifts worthy of sharing and that I must strive to use my gifts to Your glory.

Having Some Fun Now

"And all the people went up after him,
playing flutes and rejoicing greatly,
so that the ground shook with the sound."
1 KINGS 1:40

The definition of what is fun is purely relative to where it takes place. Like water fights, for instance. Hosing Dad down in the backyard when he isn't looking is so-so, but to zap him with a glass of ice water in the shower is even better. Then again, perhaps it is the reaction that one elicits from such actions, the initial high-pitched scream or something.

Life is like learning to swim—you take it a step at a time. You learn to duck your head under water for three seconds or float on your back before you are expected to do the two hundred-meter freestyle or a double-gainer off the ten-meter platform. Unfortunately, there are too many kids who never have the opportunity to have swimming lessons and must live by the "sink-or-swim" philosophy. Sometimes this method of learning works. More often it doesn't.

So. There we were. In Albuquerque. In the hotel room. Kind of. All of us, that is, except for my son, who was running, buck naked, down the hall, squealing like a pig and having a great ol' time. That's what vacations are for, isn't it? I mean, it is no fun to streak around your own house, but in a major hotel? Now that's fun!

It is also great fun for kids to swim in hotel pools. They won't step foot in the public pool back home, but, like running naked down the halls, it is an adventure, something different. And while in those pools, kids have a tendency to do dumb things.

"All right," I told my oldest as her younger sister splashed and dived at the other end of the pool and her "other" sibling waded down the pool steps. "Keep a close watch on your little brother."

"Okay."

In no time at all, the little guy was working his way around the pool by holding on to the edge while his sister was watching his progress from the other side and his other sister continued to splash around in the deeper end. They were too far apart for my comfort so, since I was not dressed for lifeguard duty, I called my daughter over to where I was.

"Look," I explained, "you have to stick right behind him 'cause if he lets go, it would take you too long to get over to him."

I glanced down into the water where the only sign of my son was a little blond head about six inches below the water's surface.

"Like right NOW!" I hollered as I jumped to my feet.

My daughter reacted amazingly swiftly and beat me to him by about a second. She hefted him, spluttering and wiping his eyes, out of the water, fortunately no worse for his underwater adventure.

"Gotcha, Dad," she said as another lesson "sunk" in.

I sighed and went back to my seat at the edge of the pool to watch the two kids when it suddenly dawned on me that I had three kids. I was half out of my chair when the water exploded in front of me as my missing child made an emergency surface, drenching me in the process.

"Did you see that?" she exclaimed breathlessly. "I can swim all the way across underwater!"

I collapsed back into my chair and mumbled, "That's nice, dear," and wondered if this hotel had a defibrillator. I was probably going to need one before our stay was over. Things like that make you need a vacation from your vacation.

And when was the last time you and your family went on a trip and everyone left healthy and arrived back home in the same condition? If you managed to pull this one off, congratulations, for I have yet to figure out the secret. I have, however, learned one thing—avoid those winding back roads with a passion. True, they may be more scenic and interesting, but they can also offer an undesired surprise.

"Let's take the scenic route," I suggested.

"Are you sure about that?" asked my wife as she glanced toward the kids in the back of the van.

"Sure! It'll be fun."

I took the next exit off the interstate, the one marked "Family Tour Route."

"Dad—I don't feel good," a child informed me a half hour later as we threaded our way through the rugged mountains toward Taos.

"Neither do I," wailed a second.

Fine. So I started taking a lot of scenic pull-offs as my copilot searched the glove box for the ginger crystals that are supposed to help keep kids from getting carsick. I think that is because it makes them throw up immediately because of the taste—kind of like the old Ipecac syrup you keep on the kitchen shelf. Personally, I like ginger crystals, so much so that I had eaten the ones in the glove box a month ago.

Meanwhile, in the back, the kids were arguing about who was going to lose their cookies first. My wife hurriedly passed back the little plastic garbage container we keep up front.

"My tummy feels like it's going to explode," moaned my son. The girls quickly gave the trash can to him. Just in time.

"Oh, yuck! Gross!" said one over his retching.

"I guess I don't feel that bad," said the other.

Good. They wouldn't have to share the bucket.

A few miles later I looked back and noted that the sickly one still had his head in the trash bucket. He was asleep.

I nudged my wife, who laughed at the sight as she reached for the bucket.

"Nooo!" squeaked the invalid without even opening his eyes.

We let him hang on to the thing all the way to Taos.

Shortly after that, my older daughter, who is approaching driving age, asked, "What does 'Maintenance Required' mean?"

I glanced at the dash and saw the red reminder on the instrument display. Before I could explain, my wife chimed in with, "It means your father's birthday is coming up soon."

Next time I'll let her take the kids on vacation while I stay at home and get some badly needed maintenance.

Life is not all fun and games. Neither should it be hard work and worry. You have to reach a balance, an equilibrium, of play and toil, of relaxation and study.

I don't think I've quite found that balance as I've been told I work too much and need to "lighten up," whatever that means. On the other hand, I often have to tell my kids to "stop fooling around and get to work." But work at what? There are a number of possibilities.

We would all be better off if we worked at "getting our lives in order." Like my life is not in as much order as I can get?

We'd be better off if we "put our noses to the grindstone." That sounds painful.

And you'd better "get your act together." Didn't know I was in theater.

Or we'll all be "paying the piper." My wife is the flutist

around here and she already gets paid. If you ALL would like to pay her as well, that'd be fine with me.

Lord, help me find that delicate balance in my life between work and play, constancy and growth. Help me to always be mindful of Your teachings in whatever I do and to remember to stop and smell the roses along the way.

Table Manners

*"So that you may eat and drink at
my table in my kingdom and sit on thrones,
judging the twelve tribes of Israel."*
LUKE 22:30

A lot of our family togetherness centers in the kitchen. This is for two reasons: Nightly meals are the only time we are all together for any period of time (which is probably a good thing) and everyone likes to stand around and stare at the open refrigerator as a form of depraved entertainment.

Since everyone congregates at the table at least once a day, it is just natural that some pent-up aggression and anger occasionally spill over into the mealtime routine. A recent display of sibling hostility, however, took my wife and me by surprise. Everything started off fine until one daughter turned to the other and said, "That's my shirt." An innocent enough statement.

"Uh huh."

"You're wearing my shirt. Please ask before you take my things."

"But you never let me borrow anything of yours. Besides, it was in my laundry basket."

"No, I don't think so. It was in my closet, so please," at least it was a civil discussion, "stay out of my room. And do you always have to stay home when Mom and Dad go out to eat? I'd like some private time, too, you know."

Tensions were rapidly escalating. I watched in rapt fascination.

"But YOU can drive!"

Whoa. Did I miss something here? A quantum shift of some kind? I glanced at my wife, who was staring back and forth with the conversation. I could tell she was desperately trying to remember whose shirt it really was. I looked the other way at my son, who was seeing how much bread he could stuff into his mouth at one time.

"So?" responded the elder of the combatants.

I concentrated on the design on my plate and how the steam from the broccoli wafted back and forth according to which daughter was speaking.

"So I should get more time to myself."

Was that a half-eaten roll I glimpsed sailing by? I kept my head down to avoid confrontation. Fathers are supposed to avoid confrontations—it's in our contract. Besides, I might be picked as the next target. There was a sudden clatter of dog toenails on the linoleum floor as the mutt scrambled to intercept the roll before it came to a complete stop. He loves these types of discussions.

"Well, I need time, too, you know! And you. . ." What was that sailing by—a chunk of cheddar? ". . .always have the TV turned up way too loud!"

I think the dog got that morsel of cheese before it had a chance to hit the floor.

Wow! Let's see how many hostilities we can bring out within two minutes, shall we?

"Mmmmmph," said my son as bread bulged out his cheeks and slobber dripped down his chin.

"Like you never have your stereo turned up so loud it rattles my windows?"

Whiff. Another tidbit went sailing by—this time from my son, who was gleefully getting into the action. Time to step in.

"Stop!" my wife and I said in unison. She groaned and I slid a little lower in my seat 'cause I know she hates it when we say the same thing like that.

"Jinx!" shouted my youngest daughter.

It took some time, but the problems were eventually worked out to a modicum of satisfaction on everyone's part. The girls were, for a time, content with the ensuing compromises. But the dog was happiest of all.

When most people talk of dining out, they usually don't mean with their children. I try to avoid this situation myself, but there are times when it just can't be helped. Hectic schedules, vacations, family gatherings, or whatever just seem to demand that every now and then, you eat, with the children, outside of your home. Just remember to stay calm and don't order anything for yourself and everything will be okay.

We have one or two dining establishments that have come to be our favorites. They have a selection of items that both kids and adults enjoy at a reasonable price, a children's menu, and a casual atmosphere. And they always have new waitresses or waiters, which is good. The seasoned experts take some other table. I know, for I used to wait tables in my youth and I did the same thing.

"Uh, oh. Here come the Fredricksons and their kids!" I'd rush up to the maitre d' and slip a few bucks in his hand.

"Give them to Pat, okay?" I'd whisper.

I got home from a hard day at work. I was poor, I was tired, I was hungry. I walked in the door and there was no traditional giant foam arrow flying toward me. It was eerily quiet. I checked all the rooms, but no one was home. I started to panic, imagining that my family had been kidnapped by aliens or something. Then I found the note on the kitchen table. As it turns out, they left me voice mail and, just in case I didn't check that, this note so I'd know to meet them at Chuck's restaurant. Sometimes I think my family knows me too well. I grabbed my keys and headed for the door.

Up-Chuck, I mean, Chuck's is only ten minutes away but not my favorite place to dine. I always bang my hand on the table.

I arrived in reasonable time and found the rest of my family at our traditional table. I had just sat down and greeted my family when my son, who was sitting next to me and digging ice out of his glass with his spoon, knocked his glass of water over. I saw it going in slow motion. My nearest hand, previously at rest in my lap, flew up to intercept the falling glass only to bounce painfully off the bottom of the table.

Man. You'd think I would learn by now.

"Waitress, could we have a towel over here and some more water, pleeeease? And you wouldn't happen to have Band-Aids like last time, would you?"

About then, the food came for everyone else and a menu for me. Usually, I don't order much as I can fill up pretty well on what the kids leave behind, but for some reason the liver and onion special sounded especially good to me. I placed my order and waited patiently.

"Waitress, could we have some ketchup and about a gross of napkins, pleeeease?"

Everyone else dove into their food with a reasonable zeal depending on age. The older people get, the more zealous their eating habits are. Especially if you have children. I learned from the very first child to wolf down my food within two minutes of it being set before me for I may not get another chance. The possibility that a child may suddenly become cranky/gassy/ill climbs proportionately with the combined price of the meal. A disaster is sure to happen at Cafe De Ritz while you are reasonably safe at Snarf City.

While I sat there waiting, I once again observed the eating habits of my children. I don't know where they come up with the stuff they do, but it certainly isn't from my side of the family. I never ate Jell-O with my fingers or drank hot chocolate with a straw.

Then my older daughter coughed and got red in the face. "Did you know," she managed to choke out, "that all your sinuses are connected together and if you sniff while eating carrots, the chunks go up your nose from the back side?"

"Burrrrp!" exclaimed my other daughter. "No, I didn't know that."

My son missed this fascinating interchange as he had disappeared under the table looking for his spoon. I was glad we were in a remote, dark corner.

Everyone was still snorting their food when my meal arrived.

"Eeeyuch!" they moaned. "What is that smell?!"

"Just my food. Want some?"

"Oh, Dad! That is so gross! Liver. Onions. I don't think I'm hungry anymore."

"But you have lots of good things left!"

"Really, Dad, I couldn't eat another bite after smelling that stuff."

I knew I shouldn't have ordered anything!

"Well, then, can I have your salad? And fries?"

I can't stand to see good food go to waste. That is why I weigh fifteen pounds over my optimal weight.

Then everyone got bored while I finished everything in sight. In the process, the youngest got cranky and choked because he tried to eat his sandwich while reclining on the chair. Then he managed to stuff a straw into the parmesan cheese shaker and was about to stuff the other end up his nose.

"That's it," I sarcastically encouraged. "Now take a deep breath."

My older daughter, who didn't think I should be playing this kind of a joke on her little brother, planted a painfully accurate kick to my shin under the table. With a knee-jerk reaction, I bent down to grab my injured member, again forgetting I was at a table.

Next thing I knew, my face was in my salad bowl.

My spouse was incredulous. "What are you doing?!"

"Temporary insanity! Mumps! Leg cramps! Sheesh, I don't know!" I mumbled as I picked lettuce off my beard and glared at my grinning offspring.

"Waitress, could we have an ambulance and another gross of napkins, pleeeease?"

Finally I was able to snarf the last few fries down as everyone else was putting on their coats to go. I quickly threw the usual large tip on the table and we rushed from the restaurant before anyone else had a chance to embarrass themselves.

And to top things off, I could have sworn I overheard one of the waitresses tell the hostess, "Next time give them to Pat, would you?"

Before I had children of my own, we happened to be patronizing a fine eating establishment, courtesy of my in-laws. An acquaintance of my father-in-law and his family were seated at the table next to us. Their young son had accompanied the couple. We all said hello, but the young lad, no more than five years old, got out of his seat and walked over to our table. He had a most cheerful smile as he stuck out his hand.

"Hello," he greeted me brightly. "My name is Sean Patterson. I am awfully pleased to meet you." I was dumbstruck.

If I ever had children, I wanted one just like that. What catalog carries pretrained children, anyway?

While I never did find out the name of that company, I'd like to think my children could pass minor inspection if hard-pressed. The question is, could I pass that very same inspection?

> *Lord of hosts, help me train my children to be*
> *respectful and polite in Your eyes and to Your ways.*
> *Let them know the proper way to behave, even if they*
> *don't always need to. Use my example to show them*
> *the value of good manners and how to gracefully wear*
> *humility as they brush off their mistakes.*

A-flat

*"Do not forget to entertain strangers,
for by so doing some people have
entertained angels without knowing it."*
HEBREWS 13:2

We don't entertain much. There is a very simple reason for this—we just don't have very many repeat visitors. I'm not really sure why this is, but I have my suspicions. One reason is that the kitchen calendar is usually filled to the max with prior appointments and commitments. Another is that, like most homes with younger children, our abode is not what you would particularly call a very restful place—it is generally filled with more than its share of sound, action, and peculiarities that make it a home.

We try to educate our children in the basic facts of etiquette—really we do. Unfortunately, "Don't chew with your mouth open" is a major topic of discussion around our dinner table. The excuses for this nasty little mannerism are legion.

"But then I can't breathe!"

"That's why God made noses," I replied shortly.

"But mine is all clogged up," my daughter explained.

Oh. Then, by all means, go for it.

"Do you need to blow your nose?" my wife suggested.

My daughter nodded her head in agreement and grabbed her napkin.

"Not!" my wife and I echoed in unison. I slunk down in my chair as my wife continued the lesson.

"You leave the table to blow your nose, then wash your hands before returning."

My daughter got up to follow the suggestion.

"But leave your napkin here," I hastily added.

My brother and sister-in-law, who were dining with us, grinned at our futile training efforts. I shot an apologizing look at our guests as my son started to pound on his roll.

"Why are you doing that?" I asked.

"So I don't have to open my mouth so wide?"

Just then an outbreak of stifled coughing erupted from across the table.

"Please take smaller bites."

"Mmmmphh," replied my son.

"Say again?"

"Mmmm weary ungry."

"What? You're very hungry? But if you choke on that mouthful, you'll be very dead!" I said for the umpteenth time. "And don't talk with your mouth full. Okay?"

He looked at me with a confused look and bulging

cheeks. He looked at his mother, to our honored guests, and back to me before spitting out his overloaded mouthful on his plate. I watched with amazement along with the other unbelieving folks at the table. When he was done, he said, "Okay," and started stuffing more food in.

My remaining child finished stirring her Jell-O into the mashed potatoes and gravy.

"Uh, I'm really not hungry anymore. I think I need to be excused, please. Like real soon."

That was understandable.

"What is this?" my son asked as he held up a cloth napkin.

"Oh," my brother-in-law answered for us. "That's to tie around your head so your hair doesn't get greasy from your hands."

"Cool!" my son said as he quickly tied the napkin around his head. The corner drooped down over one eye. "And how come we have a big fork and a little fork?"

"You'll be needing the other fork in just a few minutes," I explained. He gave me a quizzical look as he continued to stuff green beans into his mouth. Sure enough, not two minutes had gone by when one of his forks hit the floor.

He brightened up. "Oh, I see what you mean! Wow, you guys think of everything!"

When we were younger, we entertained more. Then the kids came along and we gradually gave up trying. I think the end of the road was after my son was born, for he was a very vocal child. He came out of the womb screaming and, well, never quite got over it.

My cousin was visiting us from out of state. It had been a long drive for her, but we were on her way home and she wanted to see the new addition to the family. I greeted her at the door and led her into the living room, where my small son lay sleeping on the floor.

"I'm sorry," she said as she glanced at the vacuum cleaner running in the corner. "I didn't mean to interrupt house cleaning."

"What was that?" I asked above the roar.

She pointed to the corner. "The vacuum. House cleaning. I'm sorry."

"I'm sorry, too," I said loudly. "I hate house cleaning."

My spouse joined us from the other room and we talked for a while as we stood over the sleeping babe. Finally, my cousin could stand it no longer.

"Uh, are you just going to leave the vacuum on?"

"Colic!" My wife shouted back. "We can't turn it off."

My poor relative looked at us like we had lost all semblance of sanity. "How can he sleep like that, with all that noise?"

"No, no, you don't understand," I tried to explain. "That's the only way he can sleep."

I led her over to the opposite corner of the room and pointed to several bare spots in the carpet.

"This," I explained, "is where the vacuum ate the carpet threads before we realized we had to disconnect the brush." My daughter waved as she wandered through the room with stereo headphones on her head and trailing the cord behind her. Mufflers for the ears. She was no dummy.

"It's the colic," I repeated, as if that would explain everything.

My poor relative was getting a decidedly wild look in her eyes. I could tell she was seriously considering grabbing up the child and fleeing the house and the crazy people in it. I sighed and walked over to the noisy machine. I could hear that high A-flat pitch that meant the bearings were starting to go. I turned it off.

A deep, reverential silence settled over the house.

My cousin let out a shuddering sigh of relief.

My son woke up. He looked around. His face had that innocent, glowing look of a healthy newborn child, then it slowly contorted into a lopsided grimace.

"Uh, oh," my wife said.

Another daughter wandered into the room with a friend. "There he is," said my daughter to her friend. "And he's gonna blow!" The children did an abrupt about-face and quickly fled the room.

"Maybe he's hungry," suggested my cousin.

"Just fed him."

"Maybe he's wet."

I checked. Dry as a summer in Wyoming.

The kid took a deep breath.

"Waaaaaaaaaaa!"

It was starting again. I picked him up. I cooed, I rocked, I walked. His mother took over. She walked, she rocked, she cooed. Nothing would stop the high-pitched wail.

"Maybe," my cousin hollered, "you should take him to the doctor."

"The doctor is the one who suggested the vacuum. Besides, they won't let us come anymore," I explained. We had already tried that route and it had worked great for a while. We'd go to the doctor and the little guy would shut up as soon as we went through the door. Like a light switch. Got so we'd just hang out there. The receptionist would ask if we had an appointment. "No." Did we need to see the doctor again? "No." We just hung out there. They finally said they would drop our outstanding charges if we would promise to not come back.

I finally gave up, wandered back over to the cooled-down vacuum cleaner and turned it on. The pitch of the abused machine permeated the house, but within a minute the tortured child was asleep again.

My cousin began to get that wild look in her eyes again.

"My!" she shouted. "Look at the time! I have to make Omaha or Chicago or someplace before it gets dark."

"We were hoping you'd spend the night."

"Does he," she jabbed a finger in the direction of the Colic Kid, "sleep at night?"

"Depends on if the vacuum holds out or not," I explained.

Her eyes got real big. She left in a hurry. It was the last time I ever saw her. Last I heard, she still hadn't had any kids of her own.

Years later, I can still hit the exact pitch of that vacuum cleaner just before the bearings went.

It was, of course, an A-flat.

It makes a difference, of course, if you invite guests who have been, or are now at, the same point in life as you are currently. It provides for a common frame of reference.

"I've had to paint every room in the house," I explained to a recent guest, "about every other year—except this one." It was the laundry room, the one place you want to make sure everyone sees. I pointed out the grubby little finger marks and dented scuffs on the wall.

"See, here she was three, and these," I pointed out a black smear from a dirty little hand, "were from when she was four."

My friend nodded his head sagely. "My," he said, "she grew quite a bit that year!"

I beamed with pride.

"Yup."

"Hey," he said, "next time you're over, remind me to show you our family room. Got some good ones to show you."

I know we have entertained many angels in our home and our lives. Some of the faces were unfamiliar, some were sad when they came, some were happy, for one reason or the other, when they left. But it doesn't matter.

Some of those faces I know I will never again see in

this life. Others, I wish I would see more often. But what really matters is that, at one time or another, they were there and that has made all the difference—if not in their lives, in ours.

Lord, bless this family with the honor of Your presence in everything we do. Help us to be charitable and of good will toward everyone we meet, angels or not. Help us to learn from them and grow in Your love because of them.

Lasting Impressions

*"So that you may become
blameless and pure,
children of God without fault
in a crooked and depraved generation,
in which you shine
like stars in the universe."*
PHILIPPIANS 2:15

It is a sad state of affairs when you get so little company that when the doorbell rings, the visitor better step aside or be trampled by the curious crowd who wants to see who is calling. If it is a current boyfriend coming to call on a daughter, however, I do prefer to be one of the first to make it to the door. I keep a baseball bat in the vicinity just for that occasion. Just sort of a subtle reminder to behave, mind you—a gentle indoctrination into the family. After all, first impressions are important and are the ones that last a lifetime.

It was Friday night and my daughter was going to go out

to the movies with (*gasp!*) a boy whom I had not yet met.

Ding-dong.

"Dad! Stay away from the door! Please, let me get it! DAD!" she screamed as she took the stairs three at a time. But I have longer legs and got a slight head start because I just happened to be closer to the stairs. I snatched the bat as I reached for the door handle.

"Ah ha! He's mine!" I yelled back.

I flung open the door and stood there, bat in hand, ready for action. A second later, my daughter crashed into me and propelled me into the wall—a perfect body check. But she came up short as she saw what I had seen a second before.

There were my Girl Scouts running down the driveway in unabashed terror. They had been in the process of delivering the cookies I had secretly ordered last month.

Had been.

I pushed past my daughter and yelled, "Wait, come back! I want my cookies!"

They didn't even slow down. I could tell they would be great candidates for the track team.

"See what you get, Dad?" she snorted as she headed back to her room. "Now you've lost your cookies!"

Oh. Right. Blame it on me.

Well, daughter dearest, I thought, *I'm going out to the garage and dig out the chain saw. We'll see what your date thinks of that!*

When the doorbell rang again ten minutes later, I was ready and waiting by the door. I pulled it open, baseball bat in one hand, chain saw in the other.

"Aha!"

There was young Mr. Date, mouth gaping, eyes wide in surprise.

Only problem was young Mr. Date's mother was standing right behind him, mouth gaping, eyes wide in surprise.

OOPS.

"Oh, hello! Glad to meet you," I stuttered.

I saw that their eyes were fixed on my weapons.

I was speechless. Fortunately (or not), my wife had been heading up from downstairs and caught the whole thing.

"Just cleaning up the living room a little," she quickly responded, knowing that someday she was going to have to explain why we kept a chain saw in the living room. "Won't you please come in? Our daughter should be here to beat on her father any second. Might be entertaining."

Later that night, my wife and I both laughed at the front door antics of the evening. And when we were done laughing, she even asked to borrow my baseball bat for a little while.

I hid it instead. Really well. I'm no dummy.

Of course, there are significant lapses in communication that are really no one person's fault. They just happen. As my youngest says, "Sometimes bad things happen and there's nothing you can do 'bout it." True also for communication. The best you can do is learn to live with the occasional blunder, apologize, and continue on. Now my older daughter is a kind soul who would never want to confront you for any indiscretions you may have committed. She has my wife, who is a tad bit better at speaking her mind, do it instead.

A prime example of this is when I was recently "volunteered" to pick up my daughter and her current beau from a movie and drive the young lad home.

"What movie theater is it at?" I casually asked.

"The big one downtown," my wife absently replied.

Now there are only two theaters in town. One is a big complex of four theaters in one large building and the other is a large, albeit ancient, building containing only one theater. Again, being male plays a role in things since we unfortunates are born with the little piece of our brain missing (so I've often been told) that readily accepts directions or clarification of the same. I thought, *Fine, must be the complex,* and headed out.

Nope. The kids' movie wasn't listed on the front marquee.

Frantically, I sped to theater number two on the other side of town. Luckily it is a small town. Daughter and boyfriend were waiting patiently outside as I pulled up. They both climbed into the backseat (I love feeling like a chauffeur) and my daughter calmly said, "Thought it was the other movie place, huh?"

I didn't give her the satisfaction of a reply.

Then the real difficulty started.

"Dad, can we get something to drink somewhere?"

"What, no drinking fountain in there?"

"MOM always takes us out for ice cream or something when she picks us up after a movie."

Well, I thought, *sure. Fine. No capital M-O-M is going to outdo me.*

"Okay. Where would you two like to go?"

"Well, MOM always takes us to Le Chef Burger Emporium for a big milkshake."

"Okay. It is rather late and your friend needs to be home soon, but we can do that."

"Except we've been there. Let's go somewhere else."

Fine. "Where do you want to go?" I prompted, trying to keep the exasperation out of my voice.

Silence.

"Hello?" I glanced in the rearview mirror. Yep, they were still there.

Boyfriend finally spoke up. "How about that Frozen Yogurt Plus place?"

Daughter: "That closed last summer."

Boyfriend: "Oh."

Silence.

Meanwhile, I was driving in the general direction of Boyfriend's home, who lives a considerable distance outside of the city limits.

"Well, hurry up and decide. Where do you want to go?"

Daughter: "How about the Ice Cream Parlor?"

Boyfriend: "Wellll. . . ."

I realized the kid was probably thinking that the Ice Cream Parlor is not a cheap place to take your date when it suddenly dawned on me that I was going to end up footing the bill anyway. I also remembered that I had maybe four dollars on my person. If I counted the loose change in the seats, maybe another thirty cents.

"Umm, that's clear across town, honey. Someplace closer, maybe?"

"Oh, Dad!"

Silence.

Gimme a break here. Last thing I want to do is drive back and forth across town on a Friday evening.

Then I got a brilliant idea. "Say, how about that nifty little ice cream and soda shop just before you leave town?" It was in the right direction, anyway. "You guys ever been there? I hear they have a mean root beer float."

Silence.

"Let's check it out!" I prompted.

A pair of mumbled affirmatives greeted my suggestion. Good thing, too, because it was just ahead. I pulled up to the door and noticed there didn't seem to be anyone around. Uh, oh. Later than I thought. It was closed.

"Ah, um, well, where to now?"

Stone-cold silence.

I frantically looked around. Nothing even close except for a McBurger across the street and Charlie's down the way.

"How about Charlie's?" I offered.

"Uh, sir, isn't that a bar?" asked my daughter's friend.

Hmm.

"Well, I'm sure we can get a soda or something there, too."

"Daaad!"

"Okay, okay." I made an executive decision. "I guess we go across the street. Nowhere else is open or appropriate unless we want to backtrack a number of miles and you two need to be getting to your respective homes soon. That all right with you guys?"

Silence. Good. Must be mutually acceptable. McBurger it was.

So we all enjoyed a milkshake (chocolate or vanilla only) and watched the night crew mop the floor and made slightly strained small talk. I even had thirty-seven cents change and didn't have to dig around under the car seats. A good decision. Then it was off to deliver Boyfriend home before his folks called out the National Guard and finally back home before M-O-M had a chance to call out the National Guard. Daughter rushed to tell her mother of her wonderful evening.

That went reasonably well, I thought.

Later, just as I started to drift off to sleep, my wife looked up from her book and said, "You shouldn't have embarrassed your daughter like that."

I was taken by surprise. "What? What did I do now?" I stammered, thinking maybe I still had the main course from supper left in my beard.

"McBurger."

"What was wrong with that? They had very efficient floor-moppers."

"Have you no sense of class? You even sat with them! I always sit at a different table, so they can be alone."

"No," I argued. "Class takes more than four dollars. Besides, I asked them where they wanted to go. And they could've sat at a different table. I didn't make them sit with me, heaven forbid!"

"Well, you should have known better," she insisted with barely hidden scorn.

"Then you pick them up next time."

"Fine." She turned off her light.

Hah! Got out of that future episode of *Twilight Zone*.

"Fine." I turned off my light.

Silence.

Then, through a barely contained laugh I heard, one last time, "McBurger. McMen."

I am not real big on impressing people. I figure if people can't accept me for what I truly am, I'm not going to worry about it—too much. I'd much rather impress my family by providing a reasonable quality of living than by trying to be a social superman.

At the same time, I feel I have an obligation to live my life to fit my beliefs. This means I try hard to be patient, kind, and loving and instill those values in others, mainly by example and, whenever possible, by the use of humor —albeit my own unique brand. As my family will readily attest, however, it is really hard to do the correct thing all the time. And what I take for humor and fun doesn't always come across to others as the same.

Just ask my children.

I pray that the impressions I leave behind will make people smile, dear Lord. I hope my children and family feel good about my role in their lives as I endeavor to be a role model for them and for others. Forgive me, though, when I do not live up to their expectations or when the pressures of daily life drag me down. Help me to be more than I am.

Used and Abused

"But I tell you,
Do not resist an evil person.
If someone strikes you on the right cheek,
turn to him the other also."
MATTHEW 5:39

I have been described by a very few individuals who do not know me very well as "good-natured." What this basically means is I take a lot of grief without getting upset. That is a role fathers must learn and accept. You will be the brunt of many practical jokes and unthinking comments. You must learn to accept this, within reason, as part of your fate. In this age of political correctness, you must not say anything offensive to people of the opposite sex or small children—but you must also accept that they reserve the right to jump on your oversized male posterior (the one with the bull's-eye painted on it) whenever the whim strikes.

The dog was sick. He was "twitterpated" or something

and came down to our bedroom at five in the morning to make sure I knew about it. I sleepily shoved him outside, thinking it was a call of nature type of thing, but he just ran around while twitching strangely and occasionally glanced nervously in my direction. Seeing he was in a certain level of distress and being somewhat concerned, I decided to sleep on the couch and allowed him the luxury of doing the same. After a few hours of fitful sleep (on both our parts), the dog seemed much his old self.

I could not say the same.

As it was a Saturday and my daughter's battered car was in dire need of replacement for the new school year, I decided it was time for some serious car shopping. After spending several hours of looking around at the limited supply of used vehicles in our price range, I realized a more serious effort would have to be made. That afternoon, daughter in tow, I drove an hour to the nearest place with a larger selection of cars.

All I really cared about was that the vehicle had a driver's side air bag. All that my daughter really cared about was that it had a "serious" sound system. A few more hours and we had picked out a reasonable clunker that could be prepped and ready for us the following weekend and met both our requirements. The vehicle looked nice and ran reasonably well but was labeled an "economy" car (which translates to "substantially underpowered").

"You realize," I explained to my daughter, "that this vehicle does not have near the acceleration your old one does."

"You mean I won't be able to win at drag racing anymore?" she innocently replied.

I bought the car.

We arrived home just in time for supper. It was at the dinner table (where else!?) that the trouble began. Everyone got it in their minds that it was "abuse Dad" night at the Stardust—and it was all the dog's fault.

"Yeah," my younger daughter was saying as she described the dog's symptoms from the previous night. "It's like he was hyper on antihistamines or something."

High on antihistamines? Like you would know?

"Everyone please take care," I suggested, "that, if you drop an aspirin or something, make sure you find it so the dog doesn't."

My wife turned and looked at me. I had a premonition of what was coming.

"Hmm, I wonder who leaves pills just lying around on the counter?" she said.

"Hey, I always pick up whatever I drop—besides they're just vitamins—good for the animal."

"Oh, yeah, right, Dad," chimed in my son, not even comprehending the issue at hand.

What? What'd I do?

"Who around here uses antihistamines?" pressed my younger daughter.

Everyone looked at me. I pled my case.

"Once in a blue moon. And I do not leave them lying around!"

"And I suppose the reason my present car is falling apart," added in my daughter, "doesn't have anything to do with the glue coming loose on everything!"

Oh, that was a low blow!

I reached for the phone.

"I think I'll just be calling the bank to cancel that ol' car loan."

"No, no!" she squealed. "I was just kidding! Hot glue is good! Glue is our friend!"

That was more like it.

"And the next time the dog is hyper, who shall I pick to sleep on the couch with him so the rest of the family can get some sleep? Eh?"

Silence. I think I made my point.

Or maybe they were just ignoring me. It's so hard to tell the difference.

It is rare that a parent does not get upset or have hurt feelings over things his or her children unknowingly say or do. We often feel bad for having to correct our children, thinking we have done something wrong or somehow gone astray in their upbringing for this to happen. We may feel guilty for not doing or saying exactly the right thing at the right time. We may feel used or unappreciated in our efforts to provide a better life for our families.

And that's okay. The kids probably feel exactly the same way. After all, you are not a human being, you are a parent. There is a big difference. Way big.

Patience and forgiveness of minor wrongs or hasty

words are critical traits for parenting and must work both ways. The important thing to remember is that, with God's help and support, your family loves you and, hopefully sooner than later, will come to know that you have done your best for them.

Hopefully.

I know that I am sometimes less than a wonderful person. I must strive harder to be patient with my children and forgive them when I feel I have been wronged. Please help me remember, Lord, that forgiveness is a two-way street and my love for my family is as unconditional as Your love for me.

Under Construction

*"The rain came down,
the streams rose,
and the winds blew
and beat against that house;
yet it did not fall,
because it had its foundation
on the rock."*
MATTHEW 7:25

I like to do things that make our home a more pleasant place to live. I want to make it a place where family and friends will want to come, a place both relaxing and peaceful. To do this, however, takes a lot of work, of which I find neither relaxation nor peace.

"We need a tree here in the backyard," my wife suggested. "Why don't you just run out and get us a little something, preferably something over twelve feet high."

Uh-huh.

"And while you're at it, don't you think the aspens in

front would look nice with a natural stone terrace around them? You know, something to accent their natural beauty. Of course, you'd have to fill it in with dirt and put in lots of wild plants to finish it off."

Uh-huh.

"And how about a little addition to the back of the house, say two rooms or so?"

Uh-huh.

When put that way, a tree and a little stone wall sounded pretty good. I started to work immediately. Thinking that the rock terrace would be the major project, I enlisted a little help from my kids.

"Girls, would you please get the wheelbarrow and go out in the prairie and bring me back the biggest rocks you can pick up?"

They looked at me like I was something that had crawled out from under one of those rocks on the prairie.

"Daaad—do we have to?"

"Yes. It'll build muscles. You'll be 'buff.' You will be the envy of all the 'American Gladiator' women."

"Can I help, too?" my youngest chirped with great enthusiasm. "Huh, can I? Can I dig with the big shovel? An' can I ride in the wheelbarrow? Pleeease?"

Hmm, I thought. *This may take longer than I expected.*

So the little guy and I went out front and started preparations while the girls disappeared with the wheelbarrow. I dug a trench to lay the rock in with my son right behind me with his toy shovel, burying what I had just dug up. Occasionally, a stray shovelful of dirt would land on my back or spray over my head. Finally we were ready for the rocks. But there were no girls and no rocks.

Fifteen minutes later, they came trudging back, obviously tuckered out from gathering so much building material. I looked in the wheelbarrow. Three medium-sized rocks and a dozen smaller ones littered the bottom. At least they were pretty rocks.

"Where's the rest?" I inquired.

"This is all we could find," they said.

"Hey, we live on the edge of the prairie. In Wyoming. Do you have any idea how many rocks are in Wyoming?" No response. "They had to blast through bedrock to put our basement in when the house was built! Why, Wyoming is made up of 94 percent rock."

They were not impressed.

"So go get me some more loads, please."

Their eyes got wide.

"More? You didn't say anything about more! How much more?"

"As many as there are hours in the day," I told them.

They shrugged their shoulders and headed back out into the wilds. They returned a half hour later with a load only slightly larger than the first. This was going to take awhile. And I needed really big rocks to lay on the bottom. A firm foundation and all that.

"More," I growled.

"But we have twenty-four rocks, like you said!"

"I meant loads of rock, not individual rocks."

Heavy sighs.

I finally gave in.

"Gimme that thing," I told them, determined to show them some real rocks.

"Can I come?" begged my helper. "I wanna ride!"

We found a lot of big, heavy rocks. We made a lot of trips, each one a little slower and a little longer than the last. That is the amazing thing about Wyoming rock—it gets heavier as the day progresses. I also discovered that the reason you wear heavy boots is so when your son pushes over a loaded wheelbarrow of stone on your feet, you aren't crippled for life.

We did this for days. I could feel the muscles in my arms swelling and the ligaments in my back slowly pulling loose from the bone.

Then came the filler for my masterpiece. It only took thirty-seven wheelbarrow trips to get enough dirt. Only. My son had a blast. For a few days, he was in kid heaven. Rocks to throw. Dirt to fling. Rides in the wheelbarrow. Who could ask for more?

Fortune smiled upon me. I only had to move the freshly planted tree in the backyard once. The prairie never missed the rocks. My chiropractor friend said my back would feel better in time. Several weeks later, I looked back and you know what? My wife had done it to me again—the yard actually did look nice. Peaceful. Relaxing.

I even discovered where the telephone line ran through the backyard. Did you know there are five wires in those cables? They really should bury those things deeper. Must be because of the bedrock.

Every year I allow myself the luxury of one new major project. Resod the backyard. Build a pond. Move the pond. Build a clubhouse.

And there are always the maintenance projects. Replace the deck railing that the dog ate. Paint the trim where the kids beat on the house with a stick. Paint the walls that have been scrubbed so many times there's no paint left. Haul the kids out of the pond. Fix the broken, shore up the weakened, replace the missing. . .

We are constantly reevaluating our earthly home and trying to make the best of it that we can. I think it is part of our earthly stewardship that we make our place of residence as solid and as pleasant as we can, inside and out. Besides, if we can't change our kids and struggle with changing ourselves, then being able to change our environment is a most personally satisfying endeavor.

I hope the things I do are pleasing to You, Lord. I will always try to do my best at whatever I attempt, even though it may sometimes seem meaningless or mundane. Help my children see that I am doing my best for them as well as for You.

Temptation

*"Brothers, if someone is
caught in a sin,
you who are spiritual should
restore him gently.
But watch yourself,
or you also may be tempted."*
GALATIANS 6:1

I'll try anything—once.

My son had taken to in-line skating like the proverbial duck to water. But at four feet in stature, he really doesn't accumulate much velocity if he should miscalculate a turn and "biff."

"Please, please, please skate with me!" he pleaded one fine day.

"I don't think so."

"Why not? Please, oh please?"

"I don't know how and I don't have any skates, anyway."

He was incredulous at the concept that there was something his father did not know how to do.

"You don't know how to skate?"

"Nope."

"Why not?"

So I had to explain once again that the disadvantage of growing up on a ranch was that the largest piece of concrete was about six feet square and usually had something large parked on it and in-line skates had not even been invented when I was a kid.

It did not slow him down for a moment.

"So try—it's easy! Please, please? You can use my sister's skates—she won't mind. And she has really big feet, too!"

I could see he really wanted his father to participate in this enjoyable activity with him. Against my better judgment, I consented to try. How hard could it be, anyway? So I forced my size ten feet into the size seven boots until my toes had bent double. This was all right as, after I buckled the skates up, I no longer had feeling below the ankles anyway.

I stood up in the driveway. Hey—it really was easy!

Except for one thing. The driveway slanted down toward the street.

I started to roll unsteadily downhill, picking up speed faster than I had thought possible. Ten feet went by quickly. Twenty even faster. The curb to the street was rapidly approaching.

But he was still up!

I made a slight adjustment to negotiate a ninety-degree turn onto the sidewalk. The skates shot forward while my posterior shot backward.

He was down!

I sat there for a stunned moment, pondering my life, as my son skated around me several times.

"Get up, Dad!" he implored. How many times had I told him the same?

A vision flashed before me, a scene from the movie classic *Bambi*. The forest fire was racing toward a wounded Bambi.

"Get up, Bambi," urged his father. "You must get up!"

I stood up.

I went down again—hard.

"Well, this was certainly fun," I moaned as I unbuckled the rogue wheels from my now size seven feet.

There comes a point in life when you know your limits but are still tempted to exceed them anyway. If you wish your children to have a semifunctional father, at least physically, you just have to say, "No."

I have yet to learn that simple rule. That is why I don't move so fast anymore. We all have our limits and recognizing them is an important part of maturity. Even so, I keep having faith that I will be all right, that I will not become seriously injured if I exceed, with all due caution, those limits.

God lets me know when I've gone too far.

Lord, sometimes I forget I am not a kid anymore and I am tempted to do things better suited to younger, more resilient bodies. I know it is far wiser to be an enthusiastic spectator and to remain whole in body and spirit for my family. Let me always know my limits and let my children graciously understand that while age has its advantages, it has a few disadvantages to consider as well.

Out of Place

*"But everything should
be done in a
fitting and orderly way."*
1 CORINTHIANS 14:40

Place, as I have come to understand it, is the ability to know where any particular object is at any given point in time relative to a set three-dimensional space contained within the fourth dimension of time. I think it is some Einsteinian thing that is connected to an obscure sixth sense, but no one is really sure.

It used to be that I couldn't remember my name from moment to moment, mainly because I didn't have to. I had a penchant for misplacing important things—like a handful of monthly bills, paid and ready to mail. That was not a good thing to do. I knew I had mailed them! How they turned up in the side pocket of the diaper bag two months later remains a mystery to this very day.

Then came children and I was forced to recall items totally disassociated with myself. Where is this, where is that, what ever happened to the thingamajig? My under-standing wife helped me out a lot, but she realized that she was becoming a crutch to my being self-sufficient. She decided after the "diaper bag" incident to do the only humane thing she could, short of shooting me.

"Find it yourself," she said.

And you know what? Eventually I did.

It has taken time, but I think I have finally developed a reasonably honed sense of place.

The first soccer game of the season was to start in twenty minutes and we had not yet left the house.

"Come on," I yelled from the doorway. "You're going to be late!"

"I can't find my shin guards!" came the panicked reply from my daughter.

Oh, swell. The kids aren't allowed to play without those things, even though I could never figure out why. So what if you get scraped up a little? Bruises build character. Rules, however, are rules. No shin guards, no play.

"Did you look in your closet?" I yelled back.

I heard frantic digging and muffled thumps as things were ejected from the closet at a great velocity.

"Nope. Not there."

"Under your bed?" I called.

"Nada."

Okay, I thought as I glanced at my watch. *Time to turn into Superdad and call up my powers of Place.* I closed my eyes and tried to block out the thumping noises coming from my daughter's room.

Now, where had I seen those things? Hmm. After the last season, they cluttered the floor in the hallway, neglected and dirty, for several days before they had mysteriously disappeared. Dirty! That's right! They had been washed and then they were in the laundry room for a week or two before they suddenly appeared on the stairway after my wife had asked my daughter to "do something with them." I could visualize those things on the stairs as they had silently greeted me for days whenever I came in the front door.

I remembered that, after some encouragement from my son, who kept tripping over them, I had finally broken down and personally delivered them to my daughter's desk, where it seemed they sat through most of the summer. Then she cleaned her room.

Ah, yes. It all came back to me in a flash. I had helped. It was not a pretty sight. There was much pain involved. The shin guards were stuffed under the bed. That had not been acceptable. They made it to the top of the dresser. Still no good. Then they were stuffed into the soccer shoes.

Uh, oh. The soccer shoes were eventually put in the outgrown clothes box when my daughter got new shoes last month. I had also been requested to take the box to Goodwill.

I headed for the garage. The box was still there. I smiled as my procrastination tendencies had, for once, paid off. I dug down and found the shoes. Sure enough, there were the infamous shin guards.

"I've got them," I called. "Let's go!"

I glanced at my watch. Less than a minute had elapsed. Sometimes I amaze myself. Except I felt a headache coming on from the exertion.

It would not have been such a hollow victory if one of the young women at the soccer match wouldn't have talked to me.

"What is your daughter's name?" she innocently asked.

I was a little flustered at having a strange woman speak to me. My mind went blank. I thought hard but apparently I had used up all my cognitive abilities in finding the shin guards. Man, I hate it when that happens.

"Rover?" I blurted out. The word just exploded from my mouth. Sounded right at the time. I dumbly pointed to my daughter as she ran by.

The woman's eyes got real big as she slowly nodded her head and backed away from me. I saw her scribble something down on a clipboard.

"I don't know why," my daughter said after her next practice, "but my coach keeps whistling at me and calling me 'Rover.' I had to tell her three times that my name wasn't 'Rover.'"

"Maybe it is some kind of position name, like 'halfback' or something," I suggested.

"Maybe." My daughter shrugged as she walked away. "But I don't think so."

You have to be careful not to be lulled into a false sense of superiority. Do something wrong as Mister Know-it-all and your kids will never forgive you. On the other hand, if you play the simple soul, then you are looked upon as some kind of genius when you do something right—like feed yourself without drooling. Besides, the kids will be more prone to helping you if you forget your name.

Won't they?

Lord, help me to be strong when strength is needed and gentle when sensitivity is called for. Let my children know that, like them, I have weaknesses and faults. I pray that my shortcomings will not prevent me from being a good father.

Do As I Say . . .

*"Calamity upon calamity will come,
and rumor upon rumor.
They will try to get a vision from the prophet;
the teaching of the law by the priest will be lost,
as will the counsel of the elders."*
EZEKIEL 7:26

The primary learning system for children is by example and you are often that example.

Sometimes it is an extremely difficult job to be consistent between your words and actions. I, personally, have found it to be a problematic process at best and must more and more rely on the old adage, "Do as I say and not as I do." Let's face it: Males have a tendency to do whatever they please, especially in their youth. That's why their insurance rates are so much higher. The words of wisdom I try to impart to my children are usually from hard-learned experience as over the years I have discovered (usually by the "pain" method of learning) the narrow boundaries of exploration.

I truly believe that people need to make mistakes to grow, at least emotionally and spiritually. If we are to learn, we all need the freedom to fail.

"Now don't you be climbing where you can't get down." While this saying is probably more prevalent in mountainous areas (like in most of the state of Wyoming), it can apply to a number of situations. As part of my love for nature, I love to climb and I want my children to be fearless—but very respectful—when they do the same. This includes simple things like "always hike with a friend and take lots of water."

When I was in my midteens, I had free run of a ranch that contained many vertical cliffs of hardpan-prehistoric mud left over from the inland seas of antiquity. This material is not the best for climbing as, unlike rock, it is unstable and crumbles underfoot easily. On one particular outing I was trying to get some unusual photos of the ranch while exercising the family dog. I had managed to partially traverse a cliff upwards and sideways only to discover the foot- and handholds had quite suddenly disappeared. When I tried to back down, I found that easing down a cliff backwards was much more difficult than pulling yourself up. I could reach up several feet. I could reach down, however, only a matter of inches before my balance shifted to a very uncomfortable level.

I was stuck.

A mile or more in the distance, I could see the ranch house. A brisk wind was blowing toward me and I knew that, even if I yelled as loud as I could, no one would ever hear me. Below me, our ranch dog sat patiently in the shade of a big rock waiting for me to come down. He obviously had better sense than I did.

"Dog," I hollered. "Go get help!"

Dog sat in the shade, tongue out and obviously ignoring me.

"Dog! Go home! Bring rope!"

He glanced up at me with a blank stare. In the fleeting moment our eyes met, I could tell no one was really home, and then the animal quickly looked away again. Obviously this canine was no descendant of Lassie.

As I hung there, plastered against the clay wall and a good eighty feet above the ground, several things popped into my mind. One: It was a long way down. I might bounce once or twice at most before going over the edge of the next cliff below me. If I was lucky, I might be able to grab the stupid dog and take him with me. Two: There were no trees to break my fall (yet another climbing rule broken). Three: I sure wish I had some water. Four: I sure wish I had an intelligent dog. Five: I sure wish I didn't have Dad's camera, like the proverbial albatross, hanging around my neck.

Dad's camera was an ancient Argus that took phenomenal pictures with perfect colors. Man, if I fell and that thing got broken, he'd kill me! I was in a worse situation than I had first imagined!

I looked up. The edge of the cliff started no more than ten feet above my head. I looked the way I had come. Every trace of handholds had disappeared. I looked to the other side. A weak-looking bump protruded out from the cliff maybe half an inch thick and about four feet away. I couldn't see anything else beyond that point. I looked down. The dog had moved off a few feet and was now definitely out of danger if I fell. Hmmm. Maybe he wasn't so dumb after all. . . .

Sweat beaded up on my brow. I had no choice. I pulled the camera strap over my head and made careful calculations. I swung the strap and catapulted the camera over the top of the cliff. I heard it hit and roll several times before it came to a stop. There was no telltale tinkle of lens glass breaking. They may find my twisted and shattered body, but at least the camera was relatively intact.

"Here, Dog!" I yelled one last time, hoping he'd come and sit right below me. If he wasn't going to help, I was taking him with me. The dog got up. Aha! Vengeance was mine! Then he walked a few feet farther away and sat back down.

That did it. I took a deep breath and stretched my left leg across the cliff face to the little blister I had seen earlier as I pushed off with my right foot. The lump held. The toe of my boot held. And just around the corner were handholds—I was saved!

It took me another ten minutes to carefully work my way to the top of the ledge. As I rolled over the top, my mouth was so dry I couldn't have spat to save my soul. I noted the camera lay only a few inches from the edge. One more roll and it would have gone over and just as likely taken me, directly below, with it.

In the shade of the cliff face in front of me sat Dog, drooling and sneering at me like I was the dumbest creature to ever walk the earth. To the side of him was a steep trail that meandered down off the side of the cliff.

Needless to say, Dad never found out about the camera—it continued to work as perfectly as ever, maybe even better. I always carried water with me after that. And the family dog still comes along—if for nothing else, to remind me there are smarter ways of doing things. Besides, they always find the easiest way down.

"Don't do that—you'll seriously hurt yourself." Pain, be it physical or emotional, is a necessary fact of life. Without it, there is no growth. Your body has nerve endings in it for a very good reason—it's called survival. Siblings can be a different kind of pain, but you learn from them, too. Things like how to hide your stuff better or negotiate smarter or run faster or fight harder.

As a child, I was naïve. I confess that nothing much has changed over the last thirty-plus years. My older brother long ago realized this weakness in me and constantly endeavored, without success, to correct the fault.

Take the "telephone incident," for example. You see, a few years back people had telephones that you had to turn a crank to get the operator's attention at some mysterious place at the other end of the line. When we graduated to modern rotary-dial phones and party lines, the old crank phone was abandoned to the garage as a toy.

What people don't realize is that when one turned the crank on these puppies, they generated enough electricity to light up most major household appliances.

One fine day my brother says to me, "Here," he says. "Take this wire and hold it in your left hand. Good. Now take this other wire and hold it in your right hand. Fine. Now hold on tight."

"Is this going to kill me?" I asked stupidly.

"No, it won't kill you," he reassured. "It's just an old telephone—how can that kill you?"

He started cranking away on the old telephone.

While the resulting current of electricity didn't leave any permanent damage to my central nervous system other than a minor facial tick, it did make me think I was a major household appliance for several days.

My mother was not nearly so naïve as I was. After thoroughly chewing out my brother, she reinforced my experience by saying, "Don't you be hanging on to strange wires!" The lesson, I admit, stuck. And strangely enough, it also generated a curiosity and resulting education about electricity that has proven quite useful over the years. I have been really conscientious to impart that same wisdom to my children with simple little admonitions like, "Don't you be puttin' that paper clip in the wall socket or you'll blow your tennis shoes off!"

"You just have to trust in God." Faith in a power greater than ourselves is an emotional necessity. No society can survive without the rules and guidelines that originate from the human belief in God. If nothing else, the discipline learned from sitting through those long church services will help you in later years when you have to sit through endless meetings at work. It never hurts to know how to pray, either. How many times have we sincerely said things like, "God, please don't let this speaker be a boring jerk. . ."? Besides, you will be better prepared to answer your kids when they ask, "Where do all the stars come from?"

"Where do all the stars come from, Daddy?" asked my daughter one evening as we sat in a chair watching the cosmos.

I opted for the easy way out.

"God made them, sweetie."

"Why?"

Maybe it wasn't the easy way out.

"Because maybe He wants us always to remember that we aren't alone? That by our seeing the beautiful night sky full of light, He is letting us know He cares?" Sounded reasonable to me.

I tensed, waiting for the next question.

"Oh."

You know what? I guess it was reasonable enough for her, too. There are some things you just can't argue with.

Much.

"How did He make them?"

"Oh, look!" I quickly exclaimed as a meteor shot across the sky. "A shooting star!"

Saved by the proverbial bell.

We all start off pretty ignorant. It is part of a parent's responsibility to share our experiences and beliefs with our children while the kids are still willing to listen to them. It also helps us to recall the really dumb things we did and, in remembering, have a little more patience when our kids do those occasional no-nos. After all, no one is perfect, least of all parents in general and fathers in particular.

Just make sure that if your offspring follow in your steps, those steps will have a solid foundation. Do not let them climb on old clay but rather solid rock.

Lord, I pray that my children will have the common sense that I have often lacked and the wisdom I have tried so hard to find. Let my example be a beacon for them just as Christ's example will always be a beacon for me.

Fresh Starts

"Jesus replied: 'Love the Lord your God with all your
heart and with all your soul and with all your mind.'
This is the first and greatest commandment.
And the second is like it:
'Love your neighbor as yourself.' "
MATTHEW 22:37–39

The beginning of a new school year was at hand, but the
summer had taken its toll. My daughters, old enough to
stay at home unsupervised, had enjoyed the freedom of the
summer with few cares—or so we thought. What we didn't
realize was that tensions between the two had been slowly
building in their leisure time. How does the saying go? Idle
hands make for muddled minds? It was apparently time for
another infamous "family chat" when my older child could
tolerate the situation no more and called for a meeting to
straighten things out.

The two wayward daughters and their (more or less)
attentive parents convened in the kitchen, the site of so
many pleasant activities. The accuser wasted no time in

coming to the point.

"My sister doesn't do squat around here!"

Okay, then. Let's not beat around the bush. Bring it all out into the open. Yessiree.

The tone was set.

"And who appointed you my legal guardian?" shot back the other.

Hmmm. True. Age does not necessarily command respect—at least it's never worked for me.

"When Mom and Dad are at work, I'm the one responsible for what goes on around here."

Hmmm. Also true. Someone has to be supreme ruler of the abode.

My wife and I listened intently as heated accusations flew back and forth across the table.

"There's always dog hair on MY towels."

That inconsiderate dog! I've warned him about that.

"YOU never put fresh toilet paper on the holder."

The dog was also supposed to take care of that—you use, you refresh, I say.

The two started in hard and heavy, so my wife, in a superb arbitrator manner, said, "One at a time! Let your sibling finish without interruption, please. You will both get equal airtime."

I attempted to add some fatherly insight.

"Well, it seems to me—"

"Excuse me!" cut in my youngest daughter. "I was speaking here."

Well, yes, by all means, excuse me, please continue.

The argument continued, back and forth.

"And SHE plays her music really loud when I'm trying to sleep in!"

"But SHE trashes the bathroom and never cleans it up!"

I tried to make a point. "Why don't you just make the dog—"

"I'm talking here, if you don't mind!" interjected the elder daughter.

So on it went, with a few debate-coaching prompts by my spouse, who gently steered the conversation in a more constructive manner.

My stomach rumbled and I noted that our traditional suppertime had come and gone.

"The house is too small. Blah, blah, blah."

"I need my own telephone line. Yak, yak, yak."

My upper GI tract grumbled loudly.

"Excuse me! I'm trying to make a point here!"

Really! Women complain because guys never express themselves and then, when we finally try to make an intelligent comment, we get shut down like a car engine with a broken crankshaft.

"Seems to me," the moderator finally interjected as she hit the issue square on, "it all boils down to respect." The girls listened intently. No one told HER she was interrupting! She calmly continued. "Respect for each other and respect for the family. Everyone just needs to be courteous and try to do things to help each other out and respect each other's individuality and opinion."

"That's right," I agreed.

"Who asked you?!" came the unanimous response. End of discussion.

The girls came away from the ordeal feeling better with their sisterhood, and newly formed resolutions for a more harmonious relationship were made.

Even though no specific complaint had concretely been settled, everyone felt better for having the opportunity to freely yell at each other in front of Mother and Father.

Whether we are five or fifty, we need to be listened to and recognized as fellow human beings (at least most of us) with needs and desires just like everyone else's. That's what anyone wants, isn't it? It boils down to loving God and common courtesy and respect for your fellow human beings. What a difficult thing to teach, how hard to practice! Yet our Savior had it indisputably right in Matthew 22:40 when He stated, "All the Law and the Prophets hang on these two commandments."

How often I have found that, by just being quiet and listening, so much can be accomplished. Many times you don't even have to speak, just nod your head and listen. Shreds of Truth sometimes come through in that process, be it simple needs from the mouths of babes or the frustrations and fears of your friends. It is one of the most difficult things for me to practice, but I can easily see how much my children appreciate it. What higher form of respect and love can you demonstrate than to put yourself aside and give nothing but a few minutes of your attention?

That is assuming, of course, that there is some "self" left at the end of the day.

Lord, help me to listen with my heart and see clearly in my mind and soul how to meet the needs of my children and family and friends—just as You lovingly do for me. Help me to better follow Your word so that I will be a better father, husband, and son.

Differences

*"For who makes you different
from anyone else?
What do you have that you did not receive?
And if you did receive it,
why do you boast as though you did not?"*
1 CORINTHIANS 4:7

Yes, Virginia, there are differences between how men tackle child rearing as opposed to how women approach parenting. Note the keywords here: "tackle" versus "approach." The methods may be very subtle or they can be quite extreme.

I used to do the "garage sale circuit" on Saturday mornings. This was in part due to the fact that my young daughter would spring wide awake and be ready for the day at about six in the morning—every morning. She was not the quietest of creatures, either. Instead of everyone getting up at that hour, I would take it upon myself to fix us some scrambled eggs and toast, get the kid dressed, and then the two of us would spend some quality time together and head off to investigate other people's treasures. By the time we returned home, my spouse would usually be up, sipping on coffee, and ready to hear about our explorations.

"Look, Mommy," my daughter excitedly bragged, holding up her prize. "I have a new stuffed bear!"

My wife looked at the raggedy toy, then at her raggedy child, then at her raggedy husband. A disapproving expression flickered across her face.

"You've been out."

"Yesss," I hesitantly affirmed. Something was not quite right with the look in her eyes.

"In public."

"Well, I suppose we were around other human beings. Technically. You know how that early morning garage sale crowd can be—a little rough."

She looked at her small daughter as she hugged the teddy bear. Stuffing drifted onto the floor.

"Her clothes don't match."

I stared hard at my daughter's green polka-dot shorts and blue-striped shirt as she turned her grape juice-stained face toward mine. I honestly could not see what the problem was. I quickly learned.

"Blue does not go with green," she recited, as if from some secret handbook on child appearance. "Polka dots are never, never allowed to be worn with stripes. Face and hands are to be clean, hair combed."

"Oh," I said, not quite comprehending but at the

same time thinking this all sounded very familiar. "Why?"

"Because you are a persona non grata."

I'd never heard my wife swear like that before. It was scary.

"Uh, what exactly does that mean, person non gracious, or whatever?"

"It means, dear husband, that you do not want to be an unacceptable person just because you and your child look like street urchins."

I was confused. I shook my head.

"Look," she patiently explained. "What is the name of the guy that lives four houses down the street?"

"How am I supposed to know—we've only lived here for six years."

"I'll tell you his name—it's 'Darla's father.' Never mind that he has a real name and a real personality, we only know him as 'Darla's father.' Actually, I think of him as 'Darla's blind father' and I tend to avoid him because he dresses his child in polka dots and stripes."

And that is why it is of the utmost importance that your children wear clothes that match. People will remember the kids and label you accordingly.

This point was driven home after we had moved to a small town in another state. The family was strolling along the picturesque village square one fine day when this large woman came rushing down the street toward us.

"Liza," she called out joyously.

"Mary," my daughter excitedly cried. She ran forward

and literally jumped into this strange woman's out-stretched arms.

My wife and I looked at each other with puzzled expressions. We had never seen this woman in our lives and she was greeting my three-year-old as a long-lost sister.

The woman swept up my daughter and carried her over to us.

"You must be Liza's mother and father," she said as she handed my daughter back to me.

Bingo. I rest my case. But fortunately, we were not "personas au gratin," or whatever, for my daughter's clothes matched. My wife had, of course, gotten her dressed that morning.

As for the mystery woman? We never quite figured out (and they wouldn't tell) how they had met, but she and my daughter were the best of friends for a long time.

Another major difference in parenting is in the preparation of food. Sounds simple, right? Au contraire, my friend.

My wife is the cook of the family. I make no bones about it. This woman makes most every meal a gastronomical delight. Her idea of a normal supper is a roast or casserole, green salad, mashed potatoes, and some delicately simmered vegetable. China is to be used most all the time. Genuine metal flatware. Napkins. My meager contribution is to clear and wash the mountain of dishes, pots, and pans from this effort.

There are, however, occasions when she cannot prepare the meal and I must fill in.

———

"Please set the table," I asked my daughter one evening as I struggled to keep various boiling pots from smoking too badly.

She looked at the table.

"Paper plates and cups? Mom doesn't like to use paper plates and cups," she reminded me.

"Yeah? Well, your mother isn't here right at the moment, is she?" I shot back. "Look at it this way, you won't have to load much in the dishwasher tonight, will you?"

She set the table without further comment.

When everyone had finally gathered around the table, the inquisition began.

"The main course," I announced as I pulled the lid off of the smoking pot. "Dogs."

Okay. The kids like dogs.

"Dad, why is one side of my hot dog black?"

Picky, picky.

"The water boiled out of the pot, okay? Just cut off that piece if you don't like the barbecue flavor."

"Please pass the buns," someone said.

"There are no buns. Here." I tossed her a sack of sandwich bread.

"Please pass the, uh, stuff in the green bowl, please," requested my eldest child.

On to the second course. I handed her the bowl. She studied its contents for several moments and then passed it on to her sister.

"What is this?" asked the inquisitive child.

"Beaten potatoes," I replied.

"You mean 'mashed' potatoes, don't you?"

"Hey, don't quibble over words. They're good for you. Try some."

"What are these little black chunks in here?"

"I miscalculated a little, okay? They're a little well done—you want to make sure your food is cooked sufficiently, don't you? Try some."

She passed the bowl to her little brother, who quickly averted his eyes from the contents as he passed it back to me.

"You guys are so picky," I lamented. "You'd think you were kids or something. Next time we'll forgo the nice supper and I'll just throw some TV dinners in the oven. How would you like that?!"

Mistake. Three hands shot into the air.

The Jell-O met with mixed reviews, as I knew it would. I usually make it with a minimum amount of water so that if it should fall on the floor, it just bounces a few times instead of making a messy splatter. And no fruit in it, either. Other family members like it almost liquid with all kinds of strange, unidentifiable things suspended in it. Some helped themselves, others did not.

Fine. On to the last course, macaroni and cheese. Everyone examined the dish with suspicion.

"Tastes like hot dogs," said my youngest.

"Didn't want to wash another pan. It's called 'recycling,' okay?"

"I like it!" he volunteered. That was good enough for the girls—if their little brother liked something, it must be really good. The kids dug in with gusto. The bowl was empty when it finally reached me.

I noticed that my son wasn't eating.

"What's wrong?" I asked.

"My hot dog is too hot," he complained.

"That is why they call it a hot dog," my daughter volunteered.

"Blow on it," I suggested.

He blew like the Big Bad Wolf. Macaroni and cheese and a fair amount of spit flew across the table. When he was close to hyperventilating a minute later, I said, "I think you've got it."

He just sat there, staring at his plate.

"Now what's wrong?"

"My food is too cold."

There is no pleasing some people. Thank goodness for microwaves.

When my wife arrived home that evening and inquired as to what everyone had for supper, the unanimous response was "mac and cheese." When she pressed for what else everyone had, my son volunteered the "Jell-O," a daughter said "half a hot dog," and the remaining child mumbled "milk."

Hey—it had worked for me! Next time I'll teach those kids a lesson, however. I'll make them eat TV dinners.

My wife has better sense than I do in most everything that relates to the children. I think that is the way with women—they have an instinctual method of child-rearing that far transcends that of men. I'm not trying to label or promote sexism here, it's just that there are a few areas that we, as males, need to work on. Okay, I admit it, quite a few.

At the same time, there are occasions when women have to realize that accidents are going to happen and we males are going to need to be taught what is right and good for our own sake and that of our children. But, to this day, I still have not been able to comprehend what is wrong with wearing green polka-dot shorts and blue-striped shirts. I think I am just missing that gene that governs style and clothing coordination or something. Maybe that is why my wife insists on approving my attire before I leave the house every morning. Just remember, guys—jeans go with almost anything.

And I happen to like macaroni and cheese.

Lord, thank You for the strengths in our family and for our differences. Let our diversity help us grow and understand one another better so that we are able to accept and love each other to the fullest.

Falling Apart

*"One who was there had been
an invalid for thirty-eight years."*
JOHN 5:5

My children give me a lot of grief, in one form or another.
That's okay—most of the time. I manage to dish out more
than my share to them, too. Give and take, that's my
motto. Still, I sometimes pray in supplication, sometimes
in thanksgiving, "What have I done to deserve this?"

It was the end of summer; school was just a few weeks
away. Chicken pox was going around at my son's daycare.

"Do you want him to come and be exposed or have
him stay at home for a few days?" our sitter asked.

"Uh, I dunno," we said. "What do you suggest?"

"Well, it is probably better that he has them before
school starts so he doesn't get them later and miss a few
weeks of school."

Was this woman wise, or what?

He went to daycare. A week later he had chicken pox.

I gave him soothing baths. I put lots of oatmeal in the baths as it is supposed to be a great thing for chicken pox and measles and poison ivy. Probably a little too much as he looked like an underdone muffin when he came out of the tub. What did I know? I wasn't used to this type of thing. He went through the whole illness like a trooper. It hardly slowed him down at all. The only side effect was that he still can't look at oatmeal without retching.

A week later, I came home from work tired and ready for a few days of vacation.

"Come," my wife said. She led me over to where my daughter was watching TV. "Look," she said. My daughter had little red spots on her face and neck.

"I thought she already had the chicken pox?"

Apparently it wasn't enough.

As I was about to leave for work the next morning, I stopped in to see how she was doing.

"Fine," she glumly answered.

"Well, you certainly look mighty fine," I snickered.

"Uh, Dad, have you looked in the mirror lately?"

"You know I have an aversion to mirrors—that old geezer in them gives me the willies."

"Maybe you should give it a try for once," she said with a tone that made me uneasy.

I went into the bathroom and stared at the little red spots that were scattered across my face. I felt a strange dizziness sweep over me.

I went to the doctor that afternoon. She had me peel off my shirt.

"Oooo," she said.

"Yeah," I said. "I've been trying to keep in shape. Vacuuming the house really gives your biceps definition."

"Would you like me to let the hospital know they can be expecting you in a few days?" she asked.

Oh.

"You," she continued, "are going to become very sick. You will think you are going to die. By the way, do you currently have all the children you want?"

"Anyone ever tell you that you have an exceptional bedside manner?" I responded.

"Please use the back door on your way out—don't want to infect those in the waiting room, now do we?"

She was nice enough to call my wife every day to see if I was still alive.

She was right about one thing, though. I thought I was going to die.

Yes, my kids give me wonderful things. As my mom used to say, "Just wait until you have kids!" Well, I now do. And I would hope that my mother has been sufficiently avenged for my own youthful exuberance.

"Dad," my daughter reminded me for the twenty-seventh time as I popped yet another aspirin. "You are old and decrepit. And when are you going to start using that hair-grow stuff?"

"Does it bother you that my hair is getting a little thin?"

"Thin!" she snorted. "Dad, I hate to tell you this, but you are bald."

That was a mean, gross exaggeration.

"And what little hair you do have is more salt than pepper."

I was starting to see a pattern here.

"And you always wear that thing around your wrist," she continued.

"Carpal tunnel," I reminded her. "And that bothers you, too? You're not the one with a bum wrist."

"And you can't see—"

"I see what I care to. Say, is it getting dark in here? Where'd you go, anyway?"

"And you can't hear."

"What?"

"I said. . .Dad!"

"I hear what I choose to hear."

"And. . ."

Boy! She wasn't going to give up! So some of us lead rougher lives than others!

"Hey, I've got a lot going for me. I'm a self-made man, okay?"

"Well, Dad," she shot back, "I guess that relieves God of a lot of responsibility."

It's called aging. She doesn't want to and she doesn't want her parents to. It's also called facing up to reality. I'd like to think I have, in some way, come to grips with my mortality. I've accepted the fact that my list of physical limitations is growing longer. As a teenager, that isn't something you want to think about, and seeing a living example of "age" every day makes it kind of hard to ignore.

That's okay. You need to think about these things. Besides, the paint may be chipped and peeling on the outside, but the home fires are still burning brightly.

Lord, help keep me young enough in mind and body and spirit to keep up with my children. Help me show them that there is nothing wrong with aging, as long as it is done well. Let them see me as I am and be happy and willing to accept what I can give them as I humbly accept what You have given me.

Unnatural Disasters

*"The mountains will bring prosperity to the people,
the hills the fruit of righteousness."*
PSALM 72:3

I sometimes wonder why I even try to plan certain activities with my kids. Invariably something happens to make even the simplest of outings a major undertaking. I suppose the main reason I go to all the trouble is that I wish to provide the opportunity for my kids to learn and enjoy the world about them. Whether they do or not is up to them. At least they can't tell me they never had the chance.

My daughter and I had backpacked into the mountains to an alpine lake nestled among the scenic snow-covered mountains. Since this was her first experience at "packing," my own backpack was considerably overweight. This became extremely evident at around the nine thousand-foot level, when the oxygen suddenly and completely disappeared.

"Rest!" I cried for the umpteenth time.

My daughter stopped and, with an appraising eye,

watched her father. She was breathing hard.

I was panting like a dog.

"You aren't getting old or something, are you, Dad?"

"Or something. It happens. But I would be most agreeable," I took a huge, wheezing breath of air, "of your taking the frying pan or water or something else of substantial weight!"

"I think you're doing fine, Dad," she replied half-heartedly.

"I thought so. Your confidence in me is greatly appreciated."

An hour later, I was feeling the climb in my back while pounding the tent stakes into the rocks. A powerful gust of wind suddenly inflated the tent like a hot-air balloon. I grabbed a tie-down line just as the stakes pulled free and I found myself hanging on for dear life as the makeshift parachute pulled me through some prickly bushes. I frantically called out for my daughter to jump on the wayward tent and deflate it before we both went into the lake.

Of course she was nowhere in sight. Or within hearing distance.

After a number of minutes of struggling with the thing, the wind suddenly died to nothing. I went sprawling backwards onto a pile of rocks. About that same instant, my daughter appeared from the general direction of the lake.

She looked down at me.

"What'cha doin', Dad?"

"Oh, just resting for a minute. What have you been doing?"

"Just throwing rocks in the water."

"That's nice. How 'bout giving me a hand with this tent?"

We set it up without further incident from the elements.

We somehow managed to spend a relaxing afternoon traversing the shore of the phenomenal little lake and fishing without success. As evening rolled around, my daughter was suddenly ravenous.

"What's for supper?" she asked.

"Trout."

"Really? You brought trout?" Then her expression darkened as realization set in. "Uh, where is it?"

I pointed to the lake.

"You have to be kidding, Dad! We haven't caught a single fish."

"Well, I thought we would."

She was about to launch into a fully justifiable tirade when I held up my hand.

"Stew. Hobo stew. My motto is 'Be Prepared,' remember?"

"Someday," she snarled, "you are going to push me too far."

"Yeah," I reflected. "I have to work harder on that."

After supper, a magical thing happened. The sun set. The lake calmed and turned into an enormous mirror. The snow-capped mountains were reflected on the water in a phenomenal display of beauty. We were absolutely alone and the silence was broken only by far-off water in a little brook and an occasional bird. I couldn't help but think even my daughter appreciated the setting as she sat on the rocks and sketched the evening. But she would never admit it. We skipped stones on the still water. We set marshmallows ablaze over the campfire. It was a very pleasant and peaceful evening.

When the sun was all the way down, it cooled off fast. As a matter of fact, it got downright cold. Even though it was August, I realized the temperature would dip to below freezing before sunrise. I had not anticipated this. Even the feeble fire didn't keep us very warm. That happens at ten thousand feet.

My daughter finally gave up feeding the fire and getting a face full of smoke and headed for the tent and her sleeping bag. I knew that wasn't going to be enough to stay very comfortable, though.

"Wait a sec," I said.

I doused the fire and slipped on a pair of old gloves.

"Okay, now hold the tent flap open."

She thought I was nuts but did as requested. I started chucking the rocks from around our fire pit into the tent. The sound of breaking plastic reminded me that the flashlight was on top of my sleeping bag. Was. There was still enough light to see that my daughter's body language was shouting, "He's gone! My father has lost it!"

"You're pushing me again, aren't you," she said flatly.

"Trust me. You trust your dear old father, don't you?"

"Not as far as I can throw you."

Oh, ye of little faith.

I arranged the hot rocks along the inside edges of the tent. When I was done, it was almost cozy in there, especially considering the amount of room they took up. But they helped us stay relatively comfortable. Until about three in the morning.

My daughter knows I function on a little different level of consciousness than she does. I think the same of her. But if nothing else was gleaned from our outing, she learned that going downhill with a pack is much easier than going up. And in the mountains, it freezes—even in August.

I like camping at remote places, beautiful little hideaways where you hardly see anyone. Sometimes you pay a price for this solitude, however.

My wife and I stumbled onto one of our favorite places many years ago, a little park with water gushing up from the ground in deep, clear pools. Little trout dart around the bottom of these pools as the water flows into a rushing stream that is bordered by great clumps of dark green watercress. Down the road is a huge pool where multiple waterfalls have carved bathtub-sized gouges into the rock. A great place to relax and go swimming in the heat of the summer. There is only one problem with the place. The hills are so interwoven with iron ore deposits that you don't want to be there during a thunderstorm.

We didn't know this.

At three in the morning, I heard the storm approaching from miles away. I knew our little tent would keep us dry. I just hoped it wouldn't wake our two-year-old daughter who was sleeping between my wife and myself.

Suddenly, the storm was upon us. The rain was heavy, but the accompanying lightning was like nothing I have ever seen before or since. It was the kind of lightning where you could hear the sizzle of electricity before you saw the flash. The constant roar of thunder was deafening. We were terrified. All I could think about were the metal tent poles sticking up into the air.

Snap, flash, BOOM! Snap, flash, BOOM!

The smell of ozone filled the air. The storm went on and on. It was both beautifully fascinating and incredibly lethal in its power. We crouched over our sleeping daughter, hoping to deflect the inevitable lightning bolt.

I thought we were going to die. Nothing like a good near-death experience to help you get closer to your Maker.

But the bolt never came. The storm eventually passed.

Just as my wife and I were drifting back to sleep, our daughter woke up and decided it was time to play. It's amazing how that works.

I couldn't complain too much, though.

It never seems to fail. Your best intentions and immaculate plans are often thrown into disarray by forces beyond your control. That is life in general. We humans have such a driving need to control our environment that we are often disappointed when things don't go exactly as planned. But that is part of the challenge, too, to overcome adversity and rise above the situation, to turn something gone wrong, a "negative" if you will, into a "positive" experience. We just need to keep in our minds the famous Scout motto, "Be Prepared."

> *Lord, let me always be mindful of the power of Your creation and the infinite strength of the forces You have set loose. Help us to appreciate what You have given us and be content to accept what we have no power to change. And, Lord, please keep us safe. Be our lightning rod and our protector in time of need. Let us be prepared for whatever this life, and the next, has in store for us.*

Boredom and Wildflowers

"My son, if you accept my words
and store up my commands within you,
turning your ear to wisdom
and applying your heart to understanding. . ."
PROVERBS 2:1–2

Interesting things happen when you least expect them to. But that's the way life is supposed to work. If everything were expected and planned, what a dull life we would all lead. It is that sense of adventure and curiosity that leads the human race to its greatness and beauty. I have come to the conclusion, however, that while boredom can be the great mind-eraser, boredom mixed with drive is the mother of invention. It's all in the mix.

"Are we going to church this morning?" asked my bleary-eyed son early one Sunday morning.

"Yes, we are," I replied firmly.

"Okay," he replied as he trotted off to get some breakfast.

That was a switch, I thought. No groans or complaining or anything. I instantly became cautious.

My suspicions grew as the little guy quietly sat in the pew, occasionally digging some paper and pencils out of his "busy bag" to draw with. I knew he also had his current favorite stuffed toy and other odds and ends in there, along with a quarter from his own allowance for the collection plate.

When communion time came, he eagerly went with us and raced down the aisle when he was done to be the first one of the family back at their seat. People smiled at his youthful exuberance and tousled his hair as he went by. They don't know him as well as I do.

I noticed a flurry of activity in our pew as I walked back to join him. He was hiding something, I could tell. I kept my eyes peeled for mischief. And sure enough, when my wife joined us and began to sit down, the little stinker whipped a "whoopee" cushion out of his bag of tricks and quickly slid it under her descending posterior. Only my well-conditioned reflexes saved us from a potentially explosive situation. I tell you, that kid never ceases to amaze me.

Then I made the mistake of thinking about the whole thing. We both ended up giggling through half of the last hymn, him thinking about what could have been and me thinking about slipping that rubber bladder under the bishop's seat some time.

There are other times, however, when the results of boredom are not so entertaining.

"Dad," my elder daughter started in as I was unloading the dishwasher late one evening. I could tell by the tone of her voice that she was peeved. Her boyfriend was over and something wasn't quite right and it was all my fault. "The VCR is broken and we were going to watch a movie."

"The VCR is broken," I repeated dumbly.

"Yeah. It doesn't work."

"How so?" I calmly asked.

"Well, the tape won't go in, but nothing will come out, either."

"Did you try the little button marked 'power'?"

She glared at me and said, "It just sits there and makes weird grinding noises."

Grinding noises?

"Turn it off," I quickly responded.

"But we were going to watch a movie!"

"Now!" I firmly repeated, thinking of little motors and plastic gears eating themselves to a smoking mush.

She got the hint and turned just as her beau wandered up the stairs from where the TV is located. He had a sheepish look on his face as he handed her a music compact disc.

"It was stuck in the VCR," he calmly explained. "But I got it out."

My opinion of the young man went up about two notches.

"It's not scratched or anything," he quickly added as he noted the blank expression on my face.

A CD. In the VCR. Connected to the TV. The

acronyms flashed through my head in a confused haze of what was supposed to go where. I reached out to take the offending object and then hunt down my mischievous son when I noted the title on the disc. The soundtrack to *Star Trek*.

My son doesn't like *Star Trek*.

My younger daughter does.

Like the jammed VCR, wheels ground and motors whirred in my tired mind.

"Oh, sweetie-pie!" I sang out.

"Sweetie-pie" rounded the corner from her room a moment later.

"Yes?" she asked innocently.

"I believe this is yours."

"Uh, yes, it is, thanks."

"You wouldn't happen to know what it was doing in the VCR, would you?"

"Uh, I guess I forgot it was in there?"

Why did this answer sound like a question? It confused me. "You forgot it was in there. A CD. In the VCR. Connected to the TV."

"I wanted to see if it would play," she calmly explained.

Let's see, now. This kid was thirteen. A child of the techno-age. She can play the "Minute Waltz" in fifty seconds, flawlessly program a VCR in eight seconds, reset the screensaver password on my computer in three. And she committed a blatant act of mindless sabotage.

"And?" I prompted.

"It didn't."

"Why," I dumbly asked, "did you do that?"

"Uh," she stammered, "because I was bored?"

"And," I asked firmly, "are we going to try to play a CD—in the VCR—connected to the TV—ever again?"

"Uh, no?" She blinked twice in rapid succession, which I knew meant "maybe." And there you have it. People created the hydrogen bomb out of boredom. But I'm sure this child is destined for far greater things.

I once overheard a woman say to her companion, "I want my child to be like a rose, a beautiful flower." It was obvious that this woman hadn't lived in Wyoming. Roses are harder than anything to keep going here. I don't want a rose of a child, one that must be protected from the wind and drops its petals at the first hint of frosty weather.

I want wildflowers.

Wildflowers are hearty plants, blooming even through the late snows of spring. They surprise you by proliferating in the rockiest of soils and can be found anywhere and everywhere. While the blossoms may not be as big as those of roses, they are nonetheless beautiful and almost infinite in variety and color and quantity. The blossom remains long after those on domesticated plants have faded away.

And so it should be with children. Raise them to be strong and true, like the wildflower, to find their own way in their own time. Give them Values, Love, and Knowledge for fertilizer, water, and sun, and, if they should ever land in rocky soil, watch them take root and grow all the same. Take away Knowledge, however, and you have a common weed. Take away Values and you get a prickly thistle that not even the prairie dogs will eat. But take away Love and even the heartiest of plants wither and die from the inside out.

So it is with flowers, so it is with children.

Almighty God, we are like grass and flowers before Your greatness. I pray my children will grow and bloom in Your love and grace. Help me guide my children in Your ways and teach them how to use their talents and intelligence wisely. Please watch over them and help them spread the seeds of Your eternal garden wherever they go.

Sore Afraid

*"Be strong and take heart,
all you who hope in the LORD."*
PSALM 31:24

It was the first full day back to school for all the kids. The first experimental round with all the teachers, the first power plays with their fellow classmates. For my son, it was his first full day of school ever—it was First Grade. This day, this expectation, comes but once in your life. What a thrill, what excitement, what trepidation. Not knowing exactly what to expect can be a little scary. But a little fun, too.

The girls, being much older, knew what was coming and grumbled and groaned their way through breakfast, dreading the new school year and the homework. Not so with the little guy who struggled with his clothes, getting everything just so. The socks were the hardest. Not only was it the first day of school, it was his very first soccer practice. He wanted to wear the shin guards all day.

When I got home from work, I was anxious to hear

how things had gone. I didn't have to wait long.

"How was your day?" I asked my son, who was waiting for me by the door.

"Great!" he replied excitedly. "Can we go to soccer practice now?"

"And how was your day?" I asked my younger daughter a few moments later.

Her reply was unintelligible.

"What?" I asked, not quite catching her response.

"I said, it stunk."

Oh. I forgot. You are not supposed to ask people over twelve years of age how their day was. Still, the truth about junior high is enough to sometimes make you fear for your children's safety and well-being. I remember that period in my life well. As they say, "Been there, done that, bought the 'farm'—I mean, 'T-shirt.' "

I figured it would probably be best to not ask my older daughter about her day and headed off to soccer practice.

At the soccer practice, the coach introduced himself and filled in the parents on what to expect for the season with our little rookies while the kids kicked balls into a baseball backstop. I stood off to the side amid a number of women when an errant ball whizzed by my fragile knees. I took a step back just as another ball narrowly missed my midsection. It was almost immediately followed by a third, aimed directly in between where the other two had passed. I quickly stepped behind the backstop as one of the moms yelled "Incoming!" and the adults scattered.

It was enough to give you concern for your physical well-being.

After a successful practice, we discovered that dodging balls can work up an appetite and headed off to grab a bite of fast food. Patience has seldom been the motto for hungry children. As we stood in line, my son kept saying, "Hurry up, Dad!"

"See these people standing here?" I pointed out. "We have to wait our turn."

Remember: Everything, no matter how obscure, is your fault and/or responsibility! You have to accept that fact to be a true dad. A meteor could crash through the roof of the house and everyone would turn to you and say, "What did ya do that for?!"

The order was placed and we went to find a table and wait for the food to be slapped together. After about a minute, my son turned to me and once again said, no demanded, "Hurry up, Dad!"

I was tired, I was hungry, I was poor. My patience was almost totally gone. I quietly explained the limits of my capabilities to my unbelieving son.

It was enough to try your patience to the limits.

We arrived home just in time for me to fulfill more fatherly responsibility.

"Dad, there's a fly in my room!"

I handed a flyswatter to my daughter.

"Go for it. Have a great time."

She shot me a disgusted look and headed back to her room. "Oh, by the way, the toilet's plugged up—again."

I perked up at the words "toilet" and "plugged."

"Is it running?" I quickly asked.

"No, it's just sitting there. How should I know if it's running or not?"

Smart aleck.

I rushed into the bathroom. No water on the floor, so that was good. The trusty plunger stood by the tub, patiently awaiting my expert touch. There wasn't any water in the bowl because at least a half roll of paper had soaked it all up. I flushed and started plunging. The water rose. The thing remained plugged. The water kept rising as I frantically pumped the plunger handle to no effect.

"Ahhhh," I cried out as I ripped the top off the toilet tank and pulled up on the float. "Thar she blows!" The water stopped just as it crested over the top of the bowl.

It was enough to get the ol' adrenaline pumping.

That is life. The ups, the downs, the excitement of never knowing quite what to expect next. How boring it would be if nothing ever challenged us, if there were never anything new or different. It is in our nature as human beings and children of God to accept the challenges that He throws our way and grow by them. I just hope He doesn't throw out too many surprises at once. But I know I am stronger for the experiences and I hope my children are also. The expectation of things to come, the thrill of accepting the next new challenge, is sometimes all that keeps me going.

Behind it all, however, lies the belief that everything will turn out all right. You just have to have faith and allow the strength that comes from that to help you maintain your sanity and sense of humor. Just think of all the absolutely wonderfully fantastic things that await you! Think of all the challenges, the excitement. . . .

Then again, maybe you shouldn't.

Dear Lord, watch over us in all that we do and help us to enjoy this day and the challenges it brings. Make us strong in mind and body and spirit as we accept life's challenges with open hearts and grow closer to You through them.

(Ex) Communication

*"Do not let any unwholesome talk
come out of your mouths,
but only what is helpful for
building others up according to their needs,
that it may benefit those who listen."*
EPHESIANS 4:29

The inane conversations that children can draw you into never cease to amaze me. Especially when it comes to food. I think it safe to say that this is an area where extreme patience is required. Take for instance the Saturday when my four-year-old walked into the kitchen. I was anxiously waiting for the coffee to drip through the filter directly into my oversized mug (nothing like that first cup of mud in the morning) and looking forward to peacefully reading the paper when in came Mr. Wonder, dragging three blankets and an oversized teddy bear behind him.

"Good morning," I offered.

No response.

"I said, good morning."

Still no response as he plopped down in front of the kitchen cabinet and began to randomly pull out cereal boxes, flinging them on the floor behind him. For a moment, I panicked.

My God, the child has gone deaf, I thought. I walked over to him and nudged him in the back with my toe.

"Hello? Anybody home?"

"Where's my cereal?" he said.

"What cereal?" I prompted.

"You know, MY cereal."

At least he wasn't deaf.

"What cereal are you looking for?"

"My Koco-Krunchies."

"I don't know where it is. Would you like some help looking for it?"

"Yes, please."

That was more like it.

"Okay, scoot over so I can look, too."

He moved perhaps a centimeter and continued to paw through the cupboard.

"Excuse me, can you scoot over a little more?"

Another centimeter. I sighed and squatted down next to him when he suddenly let out a shriek that was sure to wake the rest of the family and cause closer neighbors to phone 911.

"What, what? Did I step on your toes?"

"You're on Pooh-bear! Don't get on my Pooh-bear!"

Pooh-bear, for the uninitiated, is his favorite blanket,

so called because of the Winnie-the-Pooh design on it. Messing with Pooh-bear is living on the edge, reason for sudden acts of violence and seemingly unprovoked punches in the gut or, at his height, lower (shudder) extremities. When it comes to his possessions, this child lives by the motto, "Go ahead—make my day."

"Well, if you would scoot over I wouldn't sit on your stuff," I replied. Brother. Some people's kids.

I pawed through the thoroughly ransacked cupboard. No Koco-Krunchies. Now I started to panic for real. This kid doesn't like anything but his guaranteed 100 percent artificial food replacement and if he doesn't get his daily supply of it, he goes ballistic. Not that he usually doesn't anyway.

"Oh, look!" I exclaimed, trying to draw his attention away from the missing cereal. "Raisin Flakes! You haven't had this forever! Why don't you try some right now?"

He slowly turned his head to look at me, a motion that warned "don't go there." The sinister look on his face told me he wasn't going to buy that story but that he might be more interested in taking a chunk out of my arm. I nonchalantly scooted back.

Calm, stay calm. They can smell fear.

"Where's my Koco-Krunchies?"

I tried a new tack.

"I don't know. You had them last. Where did you put them?"

Aha! I could tell by the sudden blank look on his face that I got him with that one.

"What?"

"I said, what did you do with them? You didn't eat them all, did you?"

"What?"

"I said, you didn't eat them all, did you?" Maybe it was an intermittent deafness.

"Eat what?"

"The cereal! The Koco-Krunchies! Whatever it is that you are looking for!"

"What?"

I got up stiffly from the littered floor. Fifteen boxes of cereal, I observed, and none will do. Do you know how much fifteen boxes of cereal cost? Well, enough for a down payment on a small house, I suspect. "I need some coffee. You want some coffee?"

"I don't like coffee. It stinks. I'm hungry. I want Koco-Krunchies."

"Look, kid. I don't know who you are or what you've done with my son's brain, but we don't have any!"

"Have any what?"

Oh, my. This was bad. Better redirect the conversation a little.

"Look, how 'bout I fix you some bacon and scrambled eggs."

"I don't like eggs. Toast," he said flatly.

"Okay, bacon and toast. And orange juice. How about some orange juice."

"Okay."

"Fine. Why don't you go watch something violent on

183

TV while I fix you some breakfast."

"Okay." He got up and drug his pile of comfort into the living room.

Success! I swilled down some now-cold coffee, opened the refrigerator door, and started to pull out the ingredients for a hearty feed while the television started in on some inane commercial in the next room.

"Good thing the little critter didn't want eggs, we're all out," I muttered under my breath.

OOPS.

"Daddy, I want some eggs," came the cry from the next room. Nothing wrong with this kid's hearing.

"We don't have any," I responded.

"What?"

There went the hearing again! Maybe I should try cleaning out his ears.

"We don't have any eggs! You get bacon and toast and juice."

"I don't want any butter on my bread."

"I remember. No butter. You don't like butter. Nooo butter. Nope, no butter on your toast, nosiree."

Silence except for the screams of the cartoon characters. I started fixing breakfast. Bacon, extra crisp. Toast, barely brown, no butter. Orange juice, shaken until foamy. Just the way he likes it.

"Breakfast is ready," I finally announced.

"I'm not hungry."

"What!?"

"Huh?"

"I thought you wanted bacon and toast and juice!"

"I'm full."

I walked around the corner into the living room. "How can you. . . ?"

There he sat among blankets and cracker crumbs and an empty box of saltines, oblivious to all but the cartoon.

Oh, well. I wolfed down his breakfast and sat down at the table to read the paper.

"Daddy, I'm hungry."

Man! Where were those Koco-Krunchies?

But I think I am in trouble. You see, my wife has had to learn American Sign Language for her job. This is great, but my middle child, who is as quick as a whip, has picked up ASL from her mother. The other day they were standing in the kitchen, silently conversing away, and I noticed that they were giggling and occasionally glancing in my direction.

"What are you two talking about?" I innocently inquired.

"Nothing, nothing at all." *Giggle, giggle, sign, sign.*

"Then what is so humorous over there?"

"Oh, we were just talking about what a great father you are," replied my daughter.

"Oh. And that is funny?"

"In your case," interjected my wife, "yes."

Giggle, giggle, sign, sign.

I have always spelled out things we did not want the youngest child at the time to know about ("The c-h-o-c-o-l-a-t-e is in the f-r-e-e-z-e-r"). Pig Latin also sufficed ("Ethay ocolatechay ishay inhay eezerfray"), but children pick that up too quickly. Now the kids are getting their revenge on me, with the help of their mother. What a traitor that woman is! She spelled just as much as I did! Et tu, Brute?

Tomorrow I'm going down to the library and check out a book on sign language.

Communicating with other human beings should be easy. You speak, they listen. They speak, you listen. There—that's not so hard, is it?

Yes, it is. The actual communication process goes more like this: You speak, they look at your shoes. They speak, you are wondering what is for supper.

Now take the whole process down a few more levels, where you have the same words but with different meanings based on your age and/or experience. Or yet even further where you don't have even the commonality of words.

But the root of it all is attention. How can you hear, how can you communicate and learn, if you aren't paying attention? Those in the teaching profession know what I'm talking about, as does most any parent. The "pay attention" gene doesn't mature until you are about fifty years of age (twenty-three for females) and then, for most of us, it is too late.

This book is riddled with excerpts on communication for a good reason. Getting our thoughts and ideas across to others is a very, very difficult process. You have to speak slowly, loudly, and repeat yourself a lot. Visual aids help. Body language helps. Still, you never quite know how successful you were.

Lord, You have communicated to us over and over again, hoping that we will hear and learn about Your great plan for us. Guide me as I try to pass Your message on to my loved ones. I pray that Your words will not fall on deaf ears and that our hearts and minds will always be open to Your truth.

Space—The Only Frontier

"You need to persevere so that when you have done the will of God, you will receive what he has promised."
HEBREWS 10:36

Everyone needs a place to which he can escape to for a few minutes. Without such places, parents eventually go mad and do bad things to themselves. To children, however, nothing is sacred. There is nowhere that you can't be discovered hiding out, no location free from prying eyes and ears.

The garage and my workshop there is as about as close as I can get to personal space around my house. My young son is the only one who will venture out there, and then he only does it to see what I am doing and to steal my tools when he thinks I'm not looking.

My spouse has kindly agreed to assume responsibility over the rest of the place. That's why everything in and around our house looks so nice and clean—except the garage, which is a fire hazard of scattered tools, unlabeled boxes, and unfinished projects. But I don't care. It's mine. Sometimes I get claustrophobic and clean it up a little, but that is just so I can mess it up even better with some horrendous project that I have no intention of ever finishing. At least I can look like I'm doing something important when I escape.

Occasionally I get lulled into a false sense of security and don't notice the faraway look my wife sometimes gets. She will sit in a prominent place in a room and her eyes will get a little glassy as she stares at the piano. Then I know I am in trouble.

Last Saturday I saw it happening but didn't react fast enough. I grabbed my son around the middle, whispered, "Run!" into his ear, and headed for the garage.

"You know, I think it is time for a little rearranging," my wife casually said.

Man! I'm getting slow in my old age. I should have seen it coming by her restlessness, the way she gave every piece of furniture the eye.

"Fine. Have a nice time. We'll be out in the garage."

"I don't think so."

This particular time, the piano was the problem. It didn't look good here, it made things look too crowded over there. Do you know how much a piano weighs? Do you know how hard it is to push across a carpet? Do you have any idea what it feels like to get your hand or foot stuck between a wall and a thousand pounds of wood and steel? But two hours and three pounds of sweat later, I had to admit, once again, that the living room looked very nice. My son didn't even mind—he got to ride on the furniture when it was moved.

I was tuckered out enough that I almost didn't notice that my wife had now gone into one of the kids' bedrooms and stood there, eyes glazing over.

I grabbed my son up under my arm and ran for the door.

Yes, we all need our space, a time to ourselves without interruption or distraction when we can forget the cares of our earthly life and let our mind wander. This is different from being bored as it is something we actively seek. My son actively seeks to make sure that no one else in our family is bored.

"Daddy, will you do something with me?"

"Well, I'm kind of busy at the moment," I replied as I struggled to loosen the oil drain plug on the car.

"No one will play with me."

"Why don't you see what your sisters are doing?" I suggested.

"Okay," he said.

Fifteen seconds later my oldest daughter rushed out of the door.

"Bye," she yelled. "Have to run an errand."

Hot on her heels was my wife.

"Going to the store—need anything?"

The last remaining child came running out of the door with the dog.

"Going to walk the dog," she hollered.

My son glumly wandered out of the house.

"Daddy, will you do something with me?"

I thought about the recent exodus and sighed.

"Let me finish my project and I'll do something with you," I said.

While I moaned and groaned under the car, my son fiddled with his bike. I reached for the crescent wrench to tighten a wayward bolt.

It was gone.

I looked over at my son, who was pounding on his bike with my missing wrench.

I had a sneaking suspicion that this was a precursor to how things were going to be for the rest of the afternoon.

My son followed me around the garage like a lost dog.

"Can we do something now?" he'd ask every minute or two.

"Not yet."

"When?"

"Soon."

Finally, I got the decrepit automobile put back together. My son followed me into the house and watched as I washed up.

"Now can you do something with me?"

"Now I can do something with you. What do you want to do?"

"I don't know," he said.

"Play cards?"

"No."

"Read a book?"

"That's only for bedtime."

"Play catch?"

"No."

"Ride bikes?"

"Nowhere to go."

"Practice soccer kicks?"

"You don't know the rules."

"No," I reminded him. "You make up the rules."

Don't go there, a little voice shouted; *change the subject,* it said.

The doorbell rang and my son tore off like a shot to see who was calling on us. It's a conditioned reflex to rush for the door, a Pavlovian thing, and he is very good at it.

It was a neighborhood friend.

"Can I play with Billy?" he asked.

Saved by the (door) bell.

"Sure," I said.

My wife drove up with a load of groceries a minute later and I helped carry them in. I had just set the last bag in the kitchen when a little voice caught my attention.

"Daddy, will you do something with me?"

I turned around.

"I thought you were playing with Billy?"

"He didn't want to play over here and I don't like to play at his house."

"Okay, then. What do you want to do?"

"I don't know," he said.

I sighed. It was going to be a long afternoon. And even fathers need space sometimes.

We all need our space, time to ourselves. Even Jesus took time to pray and meditate. You and I are only human; there is only so much we can do in the hours of the day allotted to us.

I, personally, have always had a problem with priorities. What is more important, the overflowing toilet or a few minutes talking with your child? Well, maybe that was a poor example.

One thing I have learned is that you can do both, to some degree. There are a lot of tasks and chores that don't require a lot of attention, that aren't mutually exclusive. I can fix the toilet, for example, and listen to a child tell me about his or her day. I can write or read and rub someone's feet. I can move furniture and give a child a ride at the same time.

Now, if the toilet is erupting like a geyser, that may require a little more attention. Chances are, no one is going to want to be in there with you anyway.

> *Lord, help me find the time for the countless things that I should do. Help me to know what is important and what can wait. Forgive me when the demands of daily life override my desires and those of my family.*

Maturity

"When I was a child,
I talked like a child,
I thought like a child,
I reasoned like a child.
When I became a man,
I put childish ways behind me."
1 CORINTHIANS 13:11

Sometimes, no matter how hard you try to put your best foot forward, something totally unexpected trips you up. Children often experience this at an early age, and it can be a traumatic learning experience. Fortunately, the older we get, the more we take this process as a given. This is called maturity.

My wife and eldest daughter had dinner out together one Friday night—you know, one of those mysterious "women sharing" things. To this day it is hard to get the details of that meal as the two get to laughing so hard that very little of the story is understandable. I guess you had to be

AN OWNER'S GUIDE TO FATHERHOOD

there. The story as I pieced it together goes like this:

There were college guys on the right, college guys on the left. My daughter was not totally oblivious to this collegiate smorgasbord of eligible young men. I believe the term used for them these days is "buff" (which originated from the description of the intelligence of Siberian water buffaloes). Anyway, the meal ended when my attractive daughter decided she needed to "freshen up." She got up from the table and took an unsteady step forward. A dozen "buff" heads turned in her direction.

My daughter paused with a twisted smile on her face, shrugged her shoulders, and continued on her way—with a very pronounced limp.

Drag.

Her right foot scraped over the floor. She covertly reached down and hit her leg with her fist.

Step.

Drag.

She slammed her hand against her leg again as her shoe made a ripping sound on the carpet. My wife watched in amazement as her normally healthy daughter had suddenly become a disabled crazy woman.

Step.

Drag.

Hit.

Step.

Drag.

Hit.

Her daughter finally disappeared into the ladies' room.

A few minutes later, she reemerged, miraculously healed of her affliction, and walked back to the table with all the dignity and nonchalance she could muster. There was no limp, no masochistic displays. Curious expressions could clearly be noted on the faces of the buffaloes around her.

"What were you doing?" asked her incredulous mother.

My daughter looked sheepish.

"My leg went to sleep!" she moaned. "I didn't realize it until I took a step. I couldn't very well just stand there with all those guys staring at me, but my leg wouldn't work, so I just kept on going."

"Did you have to beat on yourself like that?"

"I was only trying to get the feeling back—was it that obvious?"

"If you wanted any more attention, you'd have to set your hair on fire!"

Of course this story was retold with great relish at the supper table, which led to things like peas being blown out the nose, milk spewing across the table, and general mayhem. They always tell you the funniest stories when your mouth is full and then have the gall to let you know how gross you are.

But it was worth it.

I realized something in the telling of this story, however. At one point in her life, my daughter would probably have cried from the discomfort of having her leg fall asleep. At another, she would have been mortified to have such a thing happen to her with a bunch of college boys looking on. Now she just laughed it off. You see, there are various levels of maturity in our lives, levels that help define who we are and where we are going, and my daughter had just crossed over another threshold in that journey.

May I always have the maturity to be a responsible human being. Lord, help me to see what is childish and what is not, and grant me the wisdom to learn from my mistakes.

Rules and Regulations

"In this same way,
husbands ought to love their wives
as their own bodies.
He who loves his wife loves himself.
After all,
no one ever hated his own body,
but he feeds and cares for it,
just as Christ does the church—"
EPHESIANS 5:28–29

I know I cause my spouse a lot of grief. Maybe the reason she does so well with the kids is that she has had me to practice on for so many years. Still, she has patiently taught me a lot about living and the dos and don'ts of my fatherhood role. I have also learned a great many things from her that make cohabitation with other human beings a little easier—or at least a little safer. Her list of rules are almost as binding as the Ten Commandments and are supposed to be adhered to by all in our household:

Thou shalt keep the toilet seat in the prostrated position at all times lest an unknowing person fall into depravity. (Keep the lid down.)

Thou shalt cast away all edible things that have prospered with brightly colored fungi lest they maketh thee retch with misery. (Pitch the moldy food as soon as discovered.)

Thou shalt not disassemble any device that is not in need of repair or surely it shall be a great burden unto thy purse. (If it ain't broke. . .)

Thou shalt not cleaneth thine family's clothes or they shall truly become a coat of many colors. (Never wash whites with colors.)

Gird thyself well lest thee offend thy family. (Pitch those shredded jeans with the hole in the behind—and get a haircut, too!)

Go forth into the world and be of good humor for thine countenance reflects thy heart. (Don't be such a grouch.)

Praise all who do good work and seek favour in thy sight. (Thank the cook.)

Showeth affection to thine family and thine friends lest they shun thee. (It is okay to hug.)

Toucheth not the forbidden lest thine family be offended. (If it isn't yours, leave it alone.)

Keepest thine own things close to thyself and defile not thine house. (Pick up after yourself and help clean up once in awhile.)

My son has had a very separate rule drilled into his subconscious: Make sure that when you open a door there are no naked bodies on the other side. I, on the other hand, only have one rule that I try to follow but my children have yet to learn. It is a rule my brother handed down to me: He who uses a screwdriver for a hammer will soon be using a hammer for a screwdriver.

But I have another rule that I live by.

Love thy wife.

Period.

Or else.

I have heard the statistic that, if men had to do it all over again, 80 percent would marry the same woman. On the other hand, if women had the choice, only 50 percent would marry the same man. It is a scary proposition.

I started seriously considering our marital relationship when she was in labor with our last child.

The sweat flew off her brow as she suddenly twisted toward me and growled, "You did this to me!"

I didn't know how to respond.

"Well, that's nice to know," I murmured.

I don't think it was the right response.

Ever since then I have taken it upon myself to be an especially careful husband and father. If I am asked to do something, I think it is important that I try to fulfill that request—within a reasonable amount of time. And after twenty years of living with the same person, you can tell by the tone of her voice just exactly what constitutes a reasonable amount of time.

I have willingly adopted certain chores that have eventually evolved into mine alone. Things like window cleaning and garbage collecting and vacuuming and dealing with yeuchy-stinky things that make everyone else gag but don't bother me because I have a diminished sense of smell. Things ranging from major house repairs to dealing with those little surprises resulting from the cat yacking up a hair ball or bringing us a partially eaten "gift." ("Thank you, Cat. Good Cat. Bring more, Cat.")

I also realize and admit that I have relapses. I have to be reminded of certain obligations sometimes. I forget to look at the family planner (our calendar) sometimes. I get lazy and pile my junk into a drawer instead of pitching and sorting things as I should. Sometimes I even accept blame when I feel I should be blameless. Sometimes.

In return for her unlimited insight and talent and mentoring of this family that we have produced together, I figure I better do whatever I can to support my spouse. Sure, I pay a marginally larger chunk of the bills. But raising a family is an awful lot more than paying bills.

After all, more than half of this book is hers. She is the one who carried our children. She is the one who stayed home when the kids were little. She is the one who helps them with their math homework (although I did try—once).

And almost every night, when the house is quiet and the kids settled in for bed, I show her how much I love her in the best way I know how.

I rub her feet.

Lord, I happily accept the household rules imposed on me because I care deeply about my family. The rules are easy to follow and the benefits are clear. Help me to follow Your commands, dear Lord; although they are few, the rewards are great.

Dreams of Glory

"As a father has compassion on his children,
so the LORD has compassion
on those who fear him."
PSALM 103:13

Rock, rock, rock, rock, rock. . .

There are just some things you can't fix, no matter how talented you are.

"Daddy, make it better," say your little ones, with tears in their eyes. So you get out the Band-Aids and dry their faces and, whether the "owie" needed it or not, have the imagined hurt patched up and your child is off again, playing on the rock piles and riding bicycles like nothing ever happened.

Rock, rock, rock, rock. . .

Or worried faces come to you. "Please fix it," they say, and you get out your pliers or screwdrivers or glue gun or sewing needle and work for an hour on a three-dollar toy that has seen better days. But somehow, you get it functioning and/or fixed for just a little while longer.

Rock, rock, rock. . .

"It won't go anymore," you hear. You show them where the stockpile of new batteries are and, for the ninety-eleventh time, patiently show them where the batteries go in and which way they need to point.

Rock, rock. . .

"I can't get this!" they yell with frustration over their homework. So you calmly sit down next to them and look at the problem and realize things aren't the same as when you were in school. "It's okay," you calmly tell them, "we'll get your mother. She knows this stuff."

But what can you do when your daughter comes home from school and wails, "He broke up with me!" (I'm sorry, honey. There'll be another. . . .) How do you comfort a child that is mercilessly teased by schoolmates because they aren't allowed to stay up past nine in the evening, or because they don't like to wear dresses, or their hair isn't the right color, or they do well in school? (I'm sorry. They're just jealous. . .) What do you tell your child to help the hurt go away when a close pet or a family member dies? (I'm sorry. They aren't really gone. . .)

There are just some things you can't fix, no matter how hard you try.

Rock, rock, rock. . .

Oh, if I had a penny for every time I rocked in the old rocking chair with a child nestled on my lap or slung over my shoulder. It would make a substantial dent in the national debt, I'm sure. That chair has survived three children—of course it has been reupholstered three times also. It has withstood being plopped in and jumped on and tipped over and spit up on for almost every day of the last fifteen years. They don't make chairs like that anymore.

And every time I sat in that old chair and held a child in my arms, I thought, is this the one? Is this the one that will sing beautiful music or write wondrous books? Is this the one that will go to the stars? Is this the one that will cure millions, bring peace?

So you hold them and pray for them and, when at last they are asleep, you lay them down in their beds and marvel at how angelic they look compared to an hour ago when they had you screaming bloody murder because they dumped an entire bag of kitty litter down the toilet. You look down at the human race's future, cover them warmly, and quietly tip-toe out of the room.

"Waaah!"

Sigh. Maybe not this one. But you love them with all your heart anyway. Always.

We all experience trouble and sadness, some more than others. It is important that through it all there be a sense of help and comfort, that there will be someone you can always turn to. As a parent, you must be there as much as possible for your children, as God is there for us all. We need to know there is someone to turn to who will support and love us unconditionally.

No matter what, we must foster hope in our lives and those of our loved ones. Without hope, all is lost and life is a dreary chore. I have the greatest of hopes for my children. I would like to think that they still have hope for me as well.

> *Open my heart and fill it with compassion for my children. Help me to comfort them when they are troubled or worried. Help me teach them that Your love and guidance will always be with them and share with them the comfort of trusting You with our troubles.*

Tidbits

*"As the body without the spirit is dead,
so faith without deeds is dead."*
JAMES 2:26

I have E-mail. Sometimes I think this is a curse because I receive so many items that it sometimes takes me an hour or more every day to get through the more important items. Most all I receive is work related. Occasionally, a friend will send something that sticks with me for awhile. Once in awhile, I get something that is worth keeping—and worth sharing.

The problem with electronic correspondence is that things get passed around so much they tend to lose something in the passing. Reminds me of the old children's game where kids line up and a simple sentence is whispered from one to the next. When it reaches the end, it has turned into something totally different than when it started out. In the case of E-mail, the item that changes the most, or more often than not is entirely omitted, is the original author.

Even so, here are a few of the timeless gems I have received. To the originators, I apologize that I know you not. And I thank you. I hope these stories will touch your heart—and funny bone—as much as they have mine.

The Most Caring Child

Author and lecturer Leo Buscaglia once talked about a contest he was asked to judge. The purpose of the contest was to find the most caring child. The winner was a four-year-old child whose next-door neighbor was an elderly gentleman who had recently lost his wife. Upon seeing the man cry, the little boy went into the old gentleman's yard, climbed onto his lap, and just sat there. When his mother asked him what he had said to the neighbor, the little boy said, "Nothing, I just helped him cry."

What It Means to Be Adopted

Teacher Debbie Moon's first graders were discussing a picture of a family. One little boy in the picture had a different color hair than the other family members. One child suggested that he was adopted and a little girl said, "I know all about adoptions because I was adopted."

"What does it mean to be adopted?" asked another child.

"It means," said the girl, "that you grew in your mommy's heart instead of her tummy."

Discouraged?

As I was driving home from work one day, I stopped to watch a local Little League baseball game that was being played in a park near my home. As I sat down behind the bench on the first-base line, I asked one of the boys what the score was. "We're behind 14 to nothing," he answered with a smile.

"Really," I said. "I have to say you don't look very discouraged."

"Discouraged?" the boy asked with a puzzled look on his face. "Why should we be discouraged? We haven't been up to bat yet."

Roles and How We Play Them

Whenever I'm disappointed with my spot in my life, I stop and think about little Jamie Scott. Jamie was trying out for a part in a school play. His mother told me that he'd set his heart on being in it, though she feared he would not be chosen. On the day the parts were awarded, I went with her to collect him after school. Jamie rushed up to her, eyes shining with pride and excitement. "Guess what, Mom?" he shouted, and then said those words that will remain a lesson to me: "I've been chosen to clap and cheer."

A Lesson in Heart

A lesson in "heart" is my little, ten-year-old daughter, Sarah, who was born with a muscle missing in her foot and wears a brace all the time. She came home one beautiful spring day to tell me she had competed in "field day"— that's where they have lots of races and other competitive events. Because of her leg support, my mind raced as I tried to think of encouragement for my Sarah, things I could say to her about not letting this get her down—but before I could get a word out, she said, "Daddy, I won two of the races!" I couldn't believe it! And then Sarah said, "I had an advantage." Ah. I knew it. I thought she must have been given a head start. . .some kind of physical advantage. But again, before I could say anything, she said, "Daddy, I didn't get a head start. . .my advantage was I had to try harder!"

An Eye Witness Account from New York City, on a Cold Day in December. . .

A little boy about ten years old was standing before a shoe store on the roadway, barefooted, peering through the window and shivering with cold. A lady approached the boy and said, "My little fellow, why are you looking so earnestly in that window?"

"I was asking God to give me a pair of shoes," was the boy's reply.

The lady took him by the hand and went into the store and asked the clerk to get half a dozen pairs of socks for the boy. She then asked if he could give her a basin of water and a towel. He quickly brought them to her. She took the little fellow to the back part of the store and, removing her gloves, knelt down, washed his little feet, and dried them with a towel. By this time the clerk had returned with the socks. Placing a pair upon the boy's feet, she purchased him a pair of shoes. She tied up the remaining pairs of socks and gave them to him. She patted him on the head and said, "No doubt, my little fellow, you feel more comfortable now?"

As she turned to go, the astonished lad caught her by

the hand, and looking up in her face, with tears his eyes, answered the question with these words: "Are you God's Wife?"

Two Babes in a Manger

In 1994, two Americans answered an invitation from the Russian Department of Education to teach morals and ethics (based on biblical principles) in the public schools. They were invited to teach at prisons, businesses, the fire and police departments, and a large orphanage. About one hundred boys and girls who had been abandoned, abused, and left in the care of a government-run program were in the orphanage. They relate the following story in their own words:

It was nearing the holiday season, 1994, time for our orphans to hear, for the first time, the traditional story of Christmas. We told them about Mary and Joseph arriving in Bethlehem. Finding no room in the inn, the couple went to a stable, where the baby Jesus was born and placed in a manger. Throughout the story, the children and orphanage staff sat in amazement as they listened. Some sat on the edges of their stools, trying to grasp every word. Completing the story, we gave the children three small pieces of card-board to make a crude manger. Each child was given a small paper square, cut from yellow napkins I had brought with me. No colored paper was available in the city. Following instructions, the children tore the paper and carefully laid strips in the manger for straw. Small squares of flannel, cut from a worn-out nightgown an American lady was throwing away as she left Russia, were used for the baby's blanket. A doll-like baby was cut from tan felt we had brought from the United States.

The orphans were busy assembling their manger as I walked among them to see if they needed any help. All went well until I got to one table where little Misha sat. He looked to be about six years old and had finished his project. As I looked at the little boy's manger, I was startled to see not one, but two babies in the manger. Quickly, I called for the translator to ask the lad why there were two babies in the manger. Crossing his arms in front of him and looking at this completed manger scene, the child began to repeat the story very seriously. For such a young boy, who had only heard the Christmas story once, he related the happenings accurately—until he came to the part where Mary put the baby Jesus in the manger. Then Misha started to ad-lib. He made up his own ending to the story as he said, "And when Maria laid the baby in the manger, Jesus looked at me and asked me if I had a place to stay. I told him I have no mamma and I have no papa, so I don't have any place to stay. Then Jesus told me I could stay with him. But I told him I couldn't, because I didn't have a gift to give him like everybody else did. But I wanted to stay with Jesus so much, so I thought about what I had that maybe I could use for a gift. I thought maybe if I kept him warm, that would be a good gift. So I asked Jesus, 'If I keep you warm, will that be a good enough gift?' And Jesus told me, 'If you keep me warm, that will be the best gift anybody ever gave me.' So I got into the manger, and then Jesus looked at me and he told me I could stay with him—for always."

As little Misha finished his story, his eyes brimmed full of tears that splashed down his little cheeks. Putting his hand over his face, his head dropped to the table and his shoulders shook as he sobbed and sobbed. The little orphan had found someone who would never abandon nor abuse him, someone who would stay with him—FOR ALWAYS. I've learned that it's not what you have in your life, but who you have in your life that counts.

And from the Younger Members of the Congregation. . .

Dear Pastor, I know God loves everybody but He never met my sister. Yours sincerely, Arnold. *Age 8, Nashville*

Dear Pastor, Please say in your sermon that Peter Peterson has been a good boy all week. I am Peter Peterson. Sincerely, Pete. *Age 9, Phoenix*

Dear Pastor, My father should be a minister. Every day he gives us a sermon about something. *Robert Anderson, age 11*

Dear Pastor, I'm sorry I can't leave more money in the plate, but my father didn't give me a raise in my allowance. Could you have a sermon about a raise in my allowance? Love, Patty. *Age 10, New Haven*

Dear Pastor, My mother is very religious. She goes to play bingo at church every week even if she has a cold. Yours truly, Annette. *Age 9, Albany*

Dear Pastor, I would like to go to heaven someday because I know my brother won't be there. *Stephen, Age 8, Chicago*

Dear Pastor, I think a lot more people would come to your church if you moved it to Disneyland. *Loreen, Age 9, Tacoma*

Dear Pastor, I liked your sermon where you said that good health is more important than money, but I still want a raise in my allowance. Sincerely, Eleanor. *Age 12, Sarasota*

Dear Pastor, Please pray for all the airline pilots. I am flying to California tomorrow. *Laurie, Age 10, New York City*

Dear Pastor, I hope to go to heaven some day but later than sooner. Love, Ellen. *Age 9, Athens*

Dear Pastor, Please say a prayer for our Little League team. We need God's help or a new pitcher. Thank you. Alexander. *Age 10, Raleigh*

Dear Pastor, My father says I should learn the Ten Commandments. But I don't think I want to because we have enough rules already in my house. *Joshua, Age 10, South Pasadena*

Dear Pastor, Who does God pray to? Is there a God for God? Sincerely, Christopher. *Age 9, Titusville*

Dear Pastor, Are there any devils on earth? I think there may be one in my class. *Carla, Age 10, Salina*

Dear Pastor, I liked your sermon on Sunday. Especially when it was finished. *Ralph. Age 11, Akron*

Dear Pastor, How does God know the good people from the bad people? Do you tell Him or does He read about it in the newspapers? Sincerely, Marie. *Age 9, Lewiston*

My daughter sent me this one. Do you think she was trying to tell me something?

10 Simple Rules for Dating My Daughter:

Rule One: If you pull into my driveway and honk, you'd better be delivering a package because you're sure not picking anything up.

Rule Two: You do not touch my daughter in front of me. You may glance at her, so long as you do not peer at anything below her neck. If you cannot keep your eyes or hands off of my daughter, I will remove them.

Rule Three: I am aware that it is considered fashionable for boys of your age to wear their trousers so loosely that they appear to be falling off of their hips. Please don't take this as an insult, but you and all of your friends are complete idiots. Still, I want to be fair and open-minded about this issue, so I promise this compromise: You may come to the door with your underwear showing and your pants ten sizes too big, and I will not object. However, to insure that your clothes do not, in fact, come off during the course of your date with my daughter, I will take my electric stapler and fasten your trousers securely in place to your waist.

Rule Four: I'm sure you've been told that in today's world, sex without a "barrier method" of some kind can kill you. Let me elaborate: When it comes to sex, I am the barrier. Need I explain further?

Rule Five: In order for us to get to know each other, we should talk about politics, sports, and other issues of the day. Please do not do this. The only information I require from you is an indication of when you expect to have my daughter safely back at my house, and the only word I need from you on the subject is "early."

Rule Six: I have no doubt that you are a popular fellow, with many opportunities to date other girls. This is fine with me as long as it is okay with my daughter. Otherwise, once you have gone out with my little girl, you will continue to date no one but her until she is finished with you. If you make her cry, I will make you cry.

Rule Seven: As you stand in my front hallway, waiting for my daughter to appear, and one more hour goes by, do not sigh and fidget. If you want to be on time for the movie, you should not be dating. My daughter is putting on her makeup, a process that can take longer than painting the Golden Gate Bridge.

Instead of just standing there, why not do something useful, like changing the oil in my car?

Rule Eight: The following places are not appropriate for a date with my daughter:

- Places where there are beds, sofas, or anything softer than a wooden stool.
- Places where there are no parents, policemen, or nuns within eyesight.
- Places where there is darkness.

- Places where there is dancing, holding hands, or happiness.
- Places where the ambient temperature is warm enough to induce my daughter to wear shorts, midriff T-shirts, or anything other than overalls, a sweater, and a goose down parka zipped to her throat.
- Movies with a strong romantic or sexual theme are to be avoided. Movies that feature chain saws are okay. Hockey games are okay. Retirement homes are better.

Rule Nine: Do not lie to me. I may appear to be a pot-bellied, balding, middle-aged, dim-witted has-been. But on issues relating to my daughter, I am the all-knowing merciless god of your universe. If I ask you where you are going and with whom, you have one chance to tell me the truth, the whole truth, and nothing but the truth. I have a shovel and five acres behind the house. Do not trifle with me.

Rule Ten: Be afraid. Be very afraid. It takes little time for me to mistake the sound of your car in the driveway for a chopper coming in over a rice paddy outside of Hanoi. As soon as you pull up into the driveway, you should exit the car with both hands in plain sight. Speak the perimeter password, announce in a clear voice that you have brought my daughter home safely and early, then return to your car—there is no need for you to come inside. The face at the window is mine.

SUBJECT: LESSONS FROM CHILDREN

This is from a San Diego father who has identified thirty-five truths he learned from his children.

1. There is no such thing as child-proofing your house.
2. If you spray hair spray on dust bunnies and run over them with rollerblades they can ignite.
3. A four-year-old's voice is louder than two hundred adults in a crowded restaurant.
4. If you hook a dog leash over a ceiling fan, the motor is not strong enough to rotate a forty-two-pound boy wearing Pound Puppy underwear and a Superman cape.
5. It is strong enough, however, to spread paint on all four walls of a 20 by 20-foot room.
6. Baseballs make marks on ceilings.
7. When using the ceiling fan as a bat, you have to throw the ball up several times before you get a hit.
8. You should not throw baseballs up when the ceiling fan is on.
9. A ceiling fan can hit a baseball a long way.
10. The glass in windows (even double pane) doesn't stop a baseball hit by a ceiling fan.
11. When you hear the toilet flush and the words "uh-oh," it is already too late.
12. Brake fluid mixed with Clorox makes smoke—lots of it.
13. A six-year-old boy can start a fire with a flint rock even though a sixty-year-old man says it can only be done in the movies.

14. A magnifying glass can start a fire even on an overcast day.
15. If you use a waterbed as a home plate while wearing baseball shoes, it does not leak. It explodes.
16. A king-size waterbed holds enough water to fill a 2,000-square-foot house almost 4 inches deep.
17. Legos will pass through the digestive tract of a four-year-old.
18. Duplos will not.
19. Play-Doh and microwave ovens should never be used in the same sentence.
20. Superglue is forever.
21. MacGyver can teach us many things we don't want to know.
22. So can Tarzan.
23. No matter how much Jell-O you put in the pool, you still can't walk on water.
24. Pool filters do not like Jell-O.
25. VCRs do not eject PB&J sandwiches, even though TV commercials show they do.
26. Garbage bags do not make good parachutes.
27. Marbles in gas tanks make lots of noise when driving.
28. You probably don't want to know what that odor is.
29. Always look in the oven before you turn it on.
30. Plastic toys do not like ovens.
31. The fire department in San Diego has at least a five-minute response time.

32. The spin cycle on the washing machine does not make earthworms dizzy.
33. It will, however, make cats dizzy.
34. Cats throw up twice their body weight when dizzy.
35. A good sense of humor will get you through most problems in life (unfortunately, mostly in retrospect).

"Especially unto them who are of the household of faith." What child does this not address? There are children in my congregation, in everyone's lives, who put us to shame with their simple, unquestioning faith. We have so much to learn from them if we would but listen. Our lives can be so much richer from them, and it is our duty to God to make sure that theirs are the better from us. That is why I just smile when my kids say, "Oh, Dad, grow up—you are so much like a little kid sometimes!"

Lord, let me always remember that there are more children in the world than those in my own household. Let me be mindful that the children who may need my support the most are those that I know the least. Help me always to say kind words and, above all, listen. And Lord, please, bless the children, for they are our light and our future.

Last Words

> *"Finally, brothers,*
> *whatever is true, whatever is noble,*
> *whatever is right, whatever is pure,*
> *whatever is lovely,*
> *whatever is admirable—*
> *if anything is excellent or praiseworthy—*
> *think about such things."*
> PHILIPPIANS 4:8

After three kids, would I do things any differently? You bet! While each child is unique and unpredictable in his or her own way, I now realize there are a few universal things that are in perpetually short demand. I would have to say that the following ten items should be seriously considered by any caregiver.

More music—it stimulates the mind and completes vital neural paths at an early age.

Less permissiveness—define the rules and stick with them. (Hard! So hard!)

More running—there is an unrestrained joy in physical
   well-being.
Less molding—kids will never turn out the way you
   wanted them to be.
More reading—to learn about our world and the infinite
   possibilities therein.
Less television—to stimulate independent thought and
   creativity.
More love—there is no such thing as too much.
More patience—without it, you will make your children
   bitter and unforgiving.
Less junk food—healthy minds need healthy fuels.
More humor—vital to your own sanity.

My grandfather was a genuine cowboy, one of those
silent, rugged men who was so worn he even had holes in
his leather chaps. But he never gave up. Nor did my parents nor all of my ancestors who came out West to begin
with. The family ranch, testimony to this feat, has been
around for well over a hundred years, and all of us kids
were raised to persevere through adversity, to plow
through life like a blizzard over the plains. They don't
teach you about those things in school. And I have yet to
find a book on how to survive that most trying and
rewarding of all occupations, fatherhood.

Most of us do bungle through, somehow. Our children are conceived, born, and grow, God willing, into
contributing, well-adjusted, self-supporting adults. Getting
to that end is neither an easy nor straight road. There are

hills and valleys and a lot of rocks along the way. Sometimes you get mired down in the mud and sometimes you get to look up and see the breathtaking mountains all around you.

Once we had this mean little horse that my grandfather decided to break, no matter what it took to do it. The whole family gathered to watch this battle of wills. Grandad put on his spurs and got on that animal and stayed on as it bucked and kicked and jumped all over the place. We all dove for cover behind anything of substance as the contest heated up. It went on for what seemed like forever, neither man nor beast willing to give in to the other. Then those two did something I'll never forget.

That horse laid down and rolled over.

Grandad never left the saddle.

That horse rolled right over him and that old cowboy never got off. I didn't know who was going to kill whom. For a moment, I imagined Grandad suddenly standing up and the horse riding him. But when that pony stood up again—and it wasn't an easy task—Grandad was still on top. Took awhile, and he lost his hat, but he was still in charge.

When the horse got tired and the dust cleared, Grandad smiled as they trotted up to the fence.

"Wa-hoo! Did you see what that little rascal tried to do to me? Now that's some fun!" he laughed.

Humor.

Thus the most important ingredient to surviving what will probably be the toughest, most challenging and enjoyable ride of your life.

I recently attempted to assemble a toy my son had received for his birthday. In the instructions were words that made my blood run cold: "Some patience may be required. . . ." Oh great, I thought. When something starts off like that, you instinctively know you are in trouble. And, as usual, the manufacturers understated the obvious. A LOT of patience was required and, even then, the finished product didn't quite turn out as expected. Seems I left out a tiny little plastic piece, which had rolled off the table and had been immediately gobbled up by the dog.

So it is with a family. "Some patience may be required. . ." is an understatement. An unbelievable amount of commitment, hard work, and love is required and things still never turn out quite as expected.

We can just pray that the finished product is functional and durable and is something we can be proud of—even if a few little pieces have turned up missing.

Will my family be offended by this book? I most lovingly hope not. I would hope that they will all look back in twenty years and laugh at themselves or just laugh at dear misguided Dad. Just so they laugh and know that, no matter what, no matter where they are in life, they are loved. What greater purpose should we strive for than to love and to be loved and to have a good time at it while knowing that our Divine Parent loves and laughs with us?

May peace and joy be always with you.